Becoming a Wom[an of]

God's
Enough

CYNTHIA HEALD

*He who did not spare his own Son but gave
him up for us all, how will he not also with
him graciously give us all things?*
Romans 8:32, ESV

A NavPress resource published in alliance
with Tyndale House Publishers, Inc.

NavPress is the publishing ministry of The Navigators, an international Christian organization and leader in personal spiritual development. NavPress is committed to helping people grow spiritually and enjoy lives of meaning and hope through personal and group resources that are biblically rooted, culturally relevant, and highly practical.

For more information, visit www.NavPress.com.

Becoming a Woman Whose God Is Enough

Copyright © 2014 by Cynthia Heald. All rights reserved.

A NavPress resource published in alliance with Tyndale House Publishers, Inc.

Visit the author's website at www.cynthiaheald.com.

NAVPRESS and the NAVPRESS logo are registered trademarks of NavPress, The Navigators, Colorado Springs, CO. *TYNDALE* is a registered trademark of Tyndale House Publishers, Inc. Absence of ® in connection with marks of NavPress or other parties does not indicate an absence of registration of those marks.

The Team:
Don Pape, Publisher
Caitlyn Carlson, Acquisitions Editor
Jennifer Ghionzoli, Designer

Cover vintage border copyright © Vintage Style Designs/Creative Market. All rights reserved.
Cover typeface and floral illustration copyright © Lisa Glanz/Creative Market. All rights reserved.
Cover font by Laura Worthington/Creative Market. All rights reserved.
Author photo by Shelly Han Photography, copyright © 2016. All rights reserved.

For information about special discounts for bulk purchases, please contact Tyndale House Publishers at csresponse@tyndale.com or call 800-323-9400.

Cataloging-in-Publication Data is available.

ISBN 978-1-61291-634-7

Printed in the United States of America

23	22	21	20	19	18	17
10	9	8	7	6	5	

Contents

Preface

GREETINGS, DEAR FRIEND. THE STUDY you hold in your hands was written with joy mingled with tears. Joy because I was refreshed by, reminded of, and taught anew the wonderful sufficiency of God. Tears because these truths revealed my independent spirit and lack of trust and reliance upon the Lord. Why am I so inclined to take matters into my own hands? Why do I think I know what is best? Why do I seek satisfaction from the world? Why do I not believe that God is all I need?

As I have studied, I have been humbled by God's magnificence and magnanimity. I can relate to the psalmist's cry, "O LORD, what are human beings that you should notice them, mere mortals that you should think about them?" (Psalm 144:3). God is the one who gives life; God is the one who sacrifices on our behalf; God is the one who bountifully bestows grace and love. He gladly guides, protects, and provides for His flock. He is an all-sufficient Shepherd who yearns to be enough for us.

The opening quotation in the first chapter is penned by the late nineteenth-century author Hannah Whitall Smith. In it she proposes that all of God's dealings with us are meant to teach us that God is enough. At the conclusion of the study, I nodded in hearty agreement. As we move through each day and encounter irritations, difficulties, and heartbreak, God ultimately is asking us, "Am I your rock, your fortress, your strong tower?" "Do you trust Me to work all things for good?" "Do you believe that since I did not spare My own Son that I will freely give you all things?" "Am I enough for you?"

One great lesson I have learned from this study is that God *wants* to be enough for us. He wants to be our God we depend on because He desires us to experience Him in His fullness. He is a mighty God, and He longs for us to plumb His depths and be blessed by who He is. For it is only as we trust and are dependent upon the Lord that we can truly fulfill His purpose for us.

As I communicate in one of the later chapters, I write so that I can learn and grow, and this Bible study in particular has challenged me to let God be my all in all. God's Word has spoken to my heart in piercing ways concerning my pride, my little faith, my discontent, and my meager view of God.

My prayer for you is that you, too, will be challenged and brought forth into the richness and abundance of His extraordinary grace that freely gives you all things. I pray that your life will be eternally changed because you *know* that God is enough.

With love and blessings,

Cynthia Heald

Suggestions

–FOR USING THIS STUDY–

Becoming a Woman Whose God Is Enough is suitable for group or individual study and for women of all ages, either married or single.

Each chapter includes personal thoughts and reflections from the author. Use these thoughts to prompt your examination and application of the study to your own life.

Most of the questions lead you into the Bible to help you base your responses on the Word of God. Let the Scriptures speak to you personally; there is not always a right or wrong answer. Each chapter begins with a foundational Scripture passage for you to memorize. Before or after doing the chapter study you may memorize the verse in any Bible translation you choose. Write the memory verse (from your favorite version) on a card or Post-it, put it in a place where you will see it regularly, and memorize the words. Thank God for who He is and for what He is doing in your life.

A dictionary and any Bible references or commentaries can be good resources for you in answering the questions. You'll also find them helpful in any further Bible study you might do on your own.

The Father spoke:

My child, do you know that I am enough for you?

What do You mean, Father?

Am I the first one you turn to when you have a need?

Do you feel incomplete without Me?

Do you love Me more than life?

Are you content?

Am I your Shepherd, whom you follow and trust for all things needful?

Why, Father, I want to say yes, but I know all too well how easy it is for me to rely upon myself, others, or the world to satisfy my desires.

I want you to understand the great love I have for you, love expressed by the Cross. Did I not sacrifice My own Son in order to bring you into a deep, abiding relationship with Me—a relationship that is precious in My sight and is the only one that can fully satisfy your soul? Since I gave My Son, will I not also with Him freely give you all things? All My dealings with you are meant to teach you that I am enough.

Yes, Lord. I know You long to be gracious to me in every way, and I know that in You alone can I find fulfillment.

What is necessary for you to allow Me to be all that I want to be in your life?

I'm not sure, Father, but I want to know; I want to learn. You have my attention. I hinder Your work in my life when I live independently. I want You to be enough. I am weary from continually searching for completeness and contentment on my own. My prayer will be for understanding that all Your dealings with me are for the purpose of teaching me Your sufficiency.

Good. Your desire to be taught and to grow in dependence is all-important. Now take My hand and let Me guide you into My fullness in order for you to discover that indeed, I am enough.

BASIC LESSON TO BE LEARNED:

God is Enough

CHAPTER 1

GOD, THE CREATOR AND GIVER OF ALL THINGS

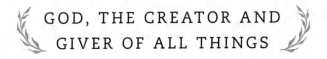

He who did not spare his own Son but gave him up for us all, how will he not also with him graciously give us all things?
ROMANS 8:32, ESV

The last and greatest lesson that the soul has to learn is the fact that God, and God alone, is enough for all its needs. This is the lesson that all His dealings with us are meant to teach; and this is the crowning discovery of our whole Christian life. GOD IS ENOUGH!
HANNAH WHITALL SMITH, *The God of All Comfort*

I BELIEVE THAT HANNAH WHITALL Smith was correct when she boldly asserted that the last and greatest lesson we must learn is the total sufficiency of God and God alone. It is last because it signifies that we have made the paramount decision to acknowledge and trust God for who He is—the supreme, everlasting, almighty God of the universe. We can thereafter rest in the power and care of our sovereign God who graciously and wisely gives us all things needful. It is the greatest lesson because our hearts are restless and our souls incomplete without the One who created us. Blaise Pascal, seventeenth-century Christian philosopher, observed, "There is a God-shaped vacuum in the heart of every man which cannot be filled by any created thing, but only by God, the Creator, made known through Jesus."[1] Until we allow God to fill this vacuum in our hearts, we will spend our lives searching for something to satisfy our emptiness. We will forfeit experiencing the fullness and richness of God's grace, presence, and plan for us. The purpose of our study is to discern the truth that only God can fulfill us and sufficiently provide what is truly necessary for our good and fulfillment. This is the ultimate lesson and one that is worth all our determination and commitment to learn—for it is, indeed, the crowning discovery of our whole Christian life.

THE GOD ABOVE ALL GODS

1. A prayer found in one of my favorite books addresses the Lord in this way: "In the beginning Thou, the Uncreated, Making all things out of nothing. . . ."[2] The first time I read these words, I was startled by the author's address to the "Uncreated," and then I realized that it is the perfect description of God—only the Uncreated could become the Creator. What further observations about God's supremacy can be learned from these verses?

PSALM 89:5-8 ....

PSALM 103:19 · ⁀

ISAIAH 44:6-8 · ⁀

DANIEL 4:34-35 · ⁀

It is God's power as Creator of everything in the universe that first and foremost establishes His claim to be the only God. No one else can perform this feat of creation. No one else can make something out of nothing.[3]   MIKE MASON

2. Revelation 4:11 tells us, "Thou art worthy, O Lord, to receive glory and honour and power: for thou hast created all things, and for thy pleasure they are and were created" (KJV). It was for God's pleasure that He created all things, and His last and most noble act of creation was man and woman—made in

His own image. Read Genesis 1:26-28 and 2:15-25. Describe God's creation and plan for His children.

3. Allen Ross commented, "Being in God's image means that humans share, though imperfectly and finitely, in God's nature, that is, in His communicable attributes (life, personality, truth, wisdom, love, holiness, justice), and so have the capacity for spiritual fellowship with Him."[4] How do these verses express God's desire to be personally involved with us?

PROVERBS 8:17

ISAIAH 55:1-3

MATTHEW 11:28-30

Thou awakest us to delight in Thy praise; for Thou madest us for Thyself, and our heart is restless, until it repose in Thee.[5] AUGUSTINE, BISHOP OF HIPPO

4. Augustine, an early Christian theologian, affirmed Pascal's thought that only God can fulfill our needs. As you consider Augustine's and Pascal's statements, record your thoughts regarding the ways you agree or disagree with their observations.

THE GOD WHO GIVES ALL THINGS

5. Because God has created us for Himself, the apostle Paul— former Pharisee and avid persecutor of Christians—boldly declared God's graciousness in Romans 8:32. Read Romans 8:31-34 and recount the truths Paul cited to support his declaration of God's lavish generosity.

*The gift of Christ was for the express purpose of opening a
door through which all other good things might pass to us.
He is the great Charter of Christian privilege, the Preacher
of peace, the Ambassador of reconciliation, the Channel of
Divine grace. . . . As we did nothing to deserve the gift of
Christ, so the lesser blessings to enrich our lives are bestowed
not according to our deserts, but according to God's free
bounty. He gives abundantly "without money and without
price." The one condition is to receive Christ. These gifts are
to be had "with Christ," or not at all.*[6]   S. R. ALDRIDGE

6. Romans 8:34 teaches us that no one can condemn us, for
   Christ died and was raised to life for us and is sitting in the
   place of honor at God's right hand, pleading for us. To understand further the magnitude of God's gift of His Son, study
   these passages and comment on the preeminence of Christ and
   the pricelessness of His sacrifice for us.

   1 CORINTHIANS 8:6

   PHILIPPIANS 2:5-11

Your salvation is only because Christ offered a full atonement. You are complete in Him and have nothing of your own to trust in. Rest only on the merits of Jesus, for He is the only ground of confidence.[7]   CHARLES H. SPURGEON

SCRIPTURAL RESPONSES TO GOD'S SUFFICIENCY

In order to illustrate how our choices reflect whether or not we believe that God is enough, each chapter will include this special section, which explores how certain men and women in Scripture exemplified their view of God's sufficiency.

When God Didn't Seem to Be Enough

EVE

In the perfect and all-sufficient Garden of Eden, Eve was persuaded by the serpent to disobey God by eating the forbidden fruit of the tree of the knowledge of good and evil. Satan convinced Eve to eat the fruit by assuring her she would not die and that she would become like God, knowing good and evil.

——————— ⟡ ———————

The woman was convinced. She saw that the tree was beautiful and its fruit looked delicious, and she wanted the wisdom it would give her. So she took some of the fruit and ate it. Then she gave some to her husband, who was with her, and he ate it, too. At that moment their eyes were opened, and they suddenly felt shame at their nakedness.

GENESIS 3:6-7

When God Was Enough

PAUL

To the church in Philippi, Paul recounted his impeccable credentials as a Pharisee:

> I was so zealous that I harshly persecuted the church. And as for righteousness, I obeyed the law without fault. I once thought these things were valuable, but now I consider them worthless because of what Christ has done. Yes, everything else is worthless when compared with the infinite value of knowing Christ Jesus my Lord. For his sake I have discarded everything else, counting it all as garbage, so that I could gain Christ and become one with him. I no longer count on my own righteousness through obeying the law; rather, I become righteous through faith in Christ.

PHILIPPIANS 3:6-9

7. Paul declared that "God himself has given us right standing with himself" (Romans 8:33). As you reflect on these passages,

comment on how the choices Eve and Paul made can instruct you in applying the truth of God's omnipotence and sufficiency.

What is "the lie" (singular) that has ruled civilization since the fall of man? It's the belief that men and women can be their own god and live for the creation and not the Creator and not suffer any consequences.[8] WARREN W. WIERSBE

 THOUGHTS AND REFLECTIONS
FROM AN OLDER WOMAN

When something is enough, it is ample—nothing else is needed. We are satisfied and we are at rest. This has been God's purpose from the beginning. He created the Garden of Eden for Adam and Eve, and they lacked nothing. But one of Satan's schemes is to make us discontent and dissatisfied. Yet God, in His sovereignty and goodness, gives His children freedom to choose. This is what Eve did—she was deceived and she chose the forbidden fruit although she had everything she needed.

It was Eve's inclination to seek "more" outside of God's will that alerts me to my own susceptibility of thinking that I can act independently of God. "Reinhold Niebuhr, a leading post–World

War II theologian, put his finger on the problem: 'The human ego assumes its self-sufficiency and self-mastery and imagines itself secure. . . . It does not recognize the contingent and dependent character of its life and believes itself to be the author of its own existence.'"[9] Unfortunately, Eve learned all too late that she could not be the author of her own existence and that her security and satisfaction could be found in her sole dependence upon God. God is the one who created all things out of nothing; He is the only one who can ever be enough.

A. W. Tozer, American pastor and author, commented, "Always He is trying to get our attention, to reveal Himself to us, to communicate with us!"[10] Perhaps He is always trying to get our attention because He wants us to know that rest and completeness can be found in Him alone. Truly God gives abundantly, "without money and without price." How it must grieve Him when we rely on ourselves or the world to procure fulfillment. I think this is one reason Paul was so willing to count everything as worthless when he encountered the living Christ. He had sought satisfaction and fulfillment on his terms by being a righteous Pharisee, but once he met Christ, he desired nothing else. Paul was in earnest when he wrote, "He who did not withhold *or* spare [even] His own Son but gave Him up for us all, will He not also with Him freely *and* graciously give us all [other] things?" (Romans 8:32, AMPCE).

Years ago while attending a banquet, I began my journey of learning Hannah Whitall Smith's "last and greatest lesson." My husband and I were seated at a table for eight people. A young single man wanted to visit with Jack and asked if he could sit next to him. Two couples, who knew each other, came to fill out our table, leaving an empty chair by me. After introductions and small talk, the salad was served and everyone began to converse, and I began to eat by myself. After a while I became self-conscious and self-focused. Surely other people seated around us noticed that no one was talking to me. The longer I sat there the more I imagined that people were whispering, "She must be unlikable and boring." I felt isolated and conspicuous.

Floundering in my self-pity, the almighty Creator of the universe abruptly and clearly disrupted my thoughts with this challenge: *Cynthia, am I enough for you?* Stunned, I meekly whispered, "Oh, yes, Lord, You are enough for me." I was surprised—first, by His apparent intimate involvement in my circumstance, and second, by His profound question. Then in my heart these provocative and penetrating questions came from the Lord:

> *Do you understand that I love you with an everlasting love? Have you comprehended that I never leave you or forsake you? Do you know that I am the First and the Last? Must you have people constantly affirming your worth? Don't you realize that I purchased you with a great price and that you are precious in My sight? Must you seek satisfaction and validation from the world? Is not My presence, My love, My grace, My purpose, My intimate knowledge of you enough?*

Overwhelmed by this holy confrontation, I sat silently. Incredibly, I thought of God's questioning of Job and of Job's modest reply, "I am nothing—how could I ever find the answers? I will cover my mouth with my hand" (Job 40:4).

So in the midst of a bustling banquet—teary-eyed, deeply humbled, yet exceedingly blessed by the everlasting God—I covered my mouth and merely nodded. My heart was flooded with the joy and peace that only the Lord can give, and I knew in a fresh and deeper way that God and God alone was enough.

God, of your goodness, give me yourself; for you are sufficient for me. I cannot properly ask anything less, to be worthy of you. If I were to ask less, I should always be in want. In you alone do I have all.[11]

JULIAN OF NORWICH

PERSONAL THOUGHTS AND REFLECTIONS

Charles H. Brent observed, "Indeed, it would seem as though the deepest truths come only in moments of profound devotional silence and contemplation."[12] Take time to be still and prepare your heart to meditate and pray over your responses to the following thoughts. (Perhaps you might want to keep a separate journal for recording your reflections for each chapter.)

8. Carefully review this chapter, noting the key Scriptures and thoughts that impressed you. Write a brief summary of what you have learned from your study.

9. How does knowing God as the sovereign Creator help you in believing that God is enough? Include any doubts or hindrances you have in accepting the sufficiency of God.

10. As you examine your daily choices, in what areas are you tempted to satisfy your own desires instead of relying on the Lord's provision?

11. Do you agree with Hannah Whitall Smith's observation that discovering God's sufficiency is the last and greatest lesson a Christian must learn? Why or why not?

12. How has this chapter helped you in viewing God as a gracious giver of all things?

13. What is one tangible way you can begin to let God be enough for you?

14. In writing to the Ephesian church, Paul was overcome with God's grace and goodness, proclaiming, "When I think of all this, I fall to my knees and pray to the Father, the Creator of everything in heaven and on earth" (Ephesians 3:14-15). After reflecting on "all this," close this chapter by praying to the Father and Creator of everything, asking that He reveal Himself to you as the one and only God who freely gives all things. Request that the Lord, in His goodness, give Himself to you and that your heart will become more and more alert to His desire "to get your attention, to reveal Himself to you, to communicate with you." Pray that you will be a willing student ready to learn this great lesson that He alone is enough for you. Thank Him for not sparing His own Son and for graciously committing to give you all you need.

When you come to Christ and become a Christian, you are not only conscious of this new life, you are conscious of a sense of satisfaction. I say that to the glory of God and of my Savior. There is nothing that I know of, that I can think of, that I can imagine, but that I find it, and more than find it, all in him. He is enough. He is more than enough. He is the All in All. He is fully satisfying.[13]

D. MARTYN LLOYD-JONES

 SCRIPTURE MEMORY

ROMANS 8:32—*He who did not spare his own Son but gave him up for us all, how will he not also with him graciously give us all things? (ESV)*

CHAPTER 2

GOD, OUR ALL-SUFFICIENT SHEPHERD

The LORD is my shepherd; I have all that I need.

PSALM 23:1

Because the Lord is my shepherd, I do not lack anything. He satisfies my needs. That is the place to which God wants to bring us. He wants us to be independently dependent upon him, to need him alone. There are really only two options in life. If the Lord is my shepherd, then I shall not want; but if I am in want, then it is obvious that the Lord is not my shepherd.

DAVID H. ROPER, *Folk Psalms of Faith*

PHILLIP KELLER, AN EXPERIENCED SHEPHERD himself, wrote in *A Shepherd Looks at Psalm 23*, "Obviously, David, in this psalm, is speaking not as the shepherd, though he was one, but as a sheep, one of the flock. He spoke with a strong sense of pride and devotion and admiration. It was as though he literally boasted aloud, 'Look at who my shepherd is—my owner—my manager!' The Lord is!"[1] Indeed, we can take pride and delight in the knowledge that when the Lord is our Shepherd, He takes responsibility for our lives. He becomes personally involved with His sheep, and He cares and provides as needed for each one individually.

When Abraham was in the act of sacrificing his son, Isaac, on an altar, God intervened and provided a ram as a substitute. Scripture tells us, "Abraham named the place Yahweh-Yireh (which means 'the LORD will provide')" (Genesis 22:14). Hannah Whitall Smith wrote, "Abraham made the grand discovery that it was one of the characteristics of Jehovah to see and provide for the needs of His people. Therefore he called Him Jehovah-jireh—the Lord will see, or the Lord will provide."[2]

Our Shepherd is Jehovah-jireh. He is wholly committed to the welfare of His flock and to meeting all their needs.

❧ GOD PROVIDES FOR OUR NEEDS

1. God is portrayed as a shepherd in both the Old and New Testaments. How is the Lord's care for us described in these verses?

    PSALM 23 ....

    ISAIAH 40:10-11 ....

    JOHN 10:1-10 ....

2. The Philippian church sent a monetary gift to the apostle Paul, which so encouraged him that he essentially said, "My Master will fully repay you; I cannot. . . . And the measure of His supply to you will be the immeasurable 'riches of His grace.'"[3] As our Good Shepherd, God is more than able to supply our needs. How do the following Scriptures confirm God's desire and ability to provide for us?

JOHN 4:5-14

EPHESIANS 1:7-8

PHILIPPIANS 4:19

3. When Paul preached in Athens, he made this statement: "He is the God who made the world and everything in it. Since he is Lord of heaven and earth, he doesn't live in man-made temples, and human hands can't serve his needs—for he has

no needs. He himself gives life and breath to everything, and he satisfies every need" (Acts 17:24-25). What specific needs of "sheep" are addressed in these verses?

PSALM 142 ....

MATTHEW 6:25-34 ....

2 PETER 1:3-4 ....

God designed the human machine to run on Himself. He Himself is the fuel our spirits were designed to burn, or the food our spirits were designed to feed on. There is no other.[4]

C. S. LEWIS

GOD DETERMINES OUR NEEDS

4. Author W. F. Adeney observed, "God will not give what we wish, but what is requisite for us. Moreover, we cannot distinguish between the real need and our idea of what we need. It is the former only that God will supply."[5] Study these Scriptures and record what necessary choices are ours in order for the Lord to meet our needs.

PSALM 34:8-10 ....

PSALM 37:3-5 ....

PSALM 84:11 ....

---------------- ⌘ ----------------

This [Psalm 84:11] is a comprehensive promise, and is
such an assurance of the present comfort of the saints that,
whatever they desire, and think they need, they may be sure
that either Infinite Wisdom sees it is not good for them or
Infinite Goodness will give it to them in due time. Let it be
our care to walk uprightly, and then let us trust God to give
us every thing that is good for us.[6]   MATTHEW HENRY

5. W. F. Adeney wrote about distinguishing between real needs
    and our ideas of what we need. Read Luke 10:38-42 and record
    how Martha's and Jesus' ideas of what she needed differed.

6. It is important to learn, as Matthew Henry reminded us, that
    we have Infinite Wisdom and Goodness as our Shepherd, and
    He knows what is best for us. How is your relationship with
    God impacted when your perceived needs are not met?

"No good thing will he withhold," *but how is this true, when God oftentimes withholds riches and honours, and health of body from men, though they walk never so uprightly; we may therefore know that honours and riches and bodily strength, are none of God's good things; they are of the number of things indifferent which God bestows promiscuously upon the just and unjust, as the rain to fall and the sun to shine. The good things of God are chiefly peace of conscience and the joy in the Holy Ghost in this life; fruition of God's presence, and vision of his blessed face in the next, and these good things God never bestows upon the wicked, never withholds from the godly, and they are all cast up in one sum where it is said, "Blessed are the pure in heart (and such are only they that walk uprightly) for they shall see God."*[7]

CHARLES H. SPURGEON

SCRIPTURAL RESPONSES TO GOD'S SUFFICIENCY

When God Didn't Seem to Be Enough

DAVID, THE KING

At one point in David's reign, he chose not to go to war with his troops. While walking on the roof of his palace, he saw a beautiful woman, Bathsheba, taking a bath. He sent messengers to bring her to the palace, and he slept with her. She became pregnant, and David, in order to protect himself, ultimately arranged for Bathsheba's husband, Uriah, to be killed in battle. The Lord sent Nathan the prophet to confront David.

The Lord, the God of Israel, says: I anointed you king of Israel and saved you from the power of Saul. I gave you your master's house and his wives and the kingdoms of Israel and Judah. And if that had not been enough, I would have given you much, much more. Why, then, have you despised the word of the Lord and done this horrible deed? For you have murdered Uriah the Hittite with the sword of the Ammonites and stolen his wife. From this time on, your family will live by the sword because you have despised me by taking Uriah's wife to be your own.

2 SAMUEL 12:7-10

When God Was Enough

DAVID, THE SHEPHERD

During King Saul's reign, the Israelite troops faced the Philistine army for battle. Goliath, a giant of a man and a Philistine champion, separated himself from the Philistine ranks and challenged the Israelites to send out one man to fight him to determine which army would be the victor. David, the young shepherd, was visiting among the troops, and he volunteered to fight. Goliath was appalled that only a youth answered his taunts, and he cursed David.

David replied to the Philistine, "You come to me with sword, spear, and javelin, but I come to you in the name of the Lord of Heaven's Armies—the God of the armies of Israel, whom you have defied. Today the Lord will conquer you, and I will kill you and cut off your head. And then I will give the dead bodies of your men to the birds and wild animals, and the whole world will know that there is a God in Israel! And everyone assembled here will know that the Lord rescues his people, but not with sword and spear. This is the Lord's battle, and he will give you to us!"

I SAMUEL 17:45-47

As you reflect on these passages, comment on the striking contrast between David's reliance upon the Lord regarding Goliath and his reliance upon himself concerning Bathsheba. What lessons can you learn from David's life about allowing God to be enough?

THOUGHTS AND REFLECTIONS FROM AN OLDER WOMAN

There is no doubt that we have a Shepherd who is committed to provide everything we need for life and godliness. He sees and He provides for our real needs as only He can see them. It is important to remember that when we fear God, reverence Him, and follow Him as our Shepherd, only then can we have the assurance of having all that is needful. Our certainty is based on Jesus being our Good Shepherd who sacrifices His life for His sheep. He is our Gate; His sacrificial death on the cross is proof of His love and commitment to us. He came to meet our primary need for spiritual water so that we never thirst again.

As we studied, our Shepherd is not obligated to meet our wants or desires. We are reminded of this truth by Eve's example of taking what she wanted rather than trusting God, even when He withheld it from her. It is essential to understand that the Lord has our best interest at heart when He denies us what we think we need. C. S. Lewis prayed, "In my ignorance I have asked for A, B, and C. But don't give me them if you foresee that they would in reality be to me either snares or sorrows."[8] Trust is at the heart of allowing the Lord to shepherd us. It is believing that if He withholds something we want, He has good reasons for doing so—reasons that we may never know or understand. We must trust in what we do know, and that is of the Lord's love and personal interest in our eternal welfare. I am always touched by the Lord's response to David's sin with Bathsheba: "I gave you your master's house and his wives and the kingdoms of Israel and Judah. And if that had not been enough, I would have given you much, much more" (2 Samuel 12:8).

Concerning Psalm 37:4, Charles Spurgeon commented, "Men who delight in God desire or ask for nothing but what will please God; hence it is safe to give them *carte blanche*."[9] In a little book on prayer Spurgeon also observed, "Lord, if what I ask for does not please You, neither would it please me. My desires are put into Your hands to be corrected."[10] Psalm 84:11 portrays the Lord God as our sun and a shield—the sun to give us life and light and a shield to *protect* us. So we commit our lives—our needs, our desires—into the care and keeping of our all-sufficient Jehovah-jireh, who is more than enough.

Early in our marriage, my husband bought a veterinary practice. On the property was a sixty-five-year-old duplex that we agreed would be our temporary dwelling until his practice was established. It was in a somewhat run-down condition with cracked wallpaper, antiquated plumbing, and very little storage. Although

I had two kitchens, they were far from modern, even in that era. In order to accommodate our three young children, I had to use one of the kitchens as a bedroom!

We lived in a relatively small central Texas town, which could boast of four major hospitals. Consequently, we soon began to meet a preponderance of doctors, who graciously invited us to their lovely, one-kitchen homes. Now I was in a quandary; I needed to reciprocate, but I was ashamed of our home.

Our stay in this less-than-desirable situation was prolonged because we did buy a piece of land and began to make plans to build. At least now I could talk about plans for our new home. As God would have it, though, we were unable to build, and finally, after four years, we bought what I called a *real* home.

During this time, my need, my desire, my *want* was a house, but the Lord saw my need in a different light. He was certainly meeting all my immediate needs. In essence, I lacked nothing for life and godliness. God knew that my real need was to learn to deal with my pride and to learn to be content with whatever my circumstances might be. Our Lord is always after the eternal, the fruit of the Spirit, the conformity to His character. He is continually transforming us into His children who reflect His nature.

At the end of the four years, as we were moving, the Lord graciously spoke to my heart: *Cynthia, I could not give you another home until you were content with the one you had. I love you too much to give you anything that will feed your pride. Your need was to learn to trust in My provision—to know that I am continually leading and working in your life in the way that is best for you. Your need was to learn to fix your eyes on Me, not on the world or its estimation of you. Your need was to know that I am enough for you.*

This insight by Annie Dillard perfectly reflects the Lord's words to me: "Your needs are absolutely guaranteed by the most stringent of warranties, in the plainest, truest words: knock; seek; ask. But you must read the fine print. 'Not as the world giveth, give I unto you'"[11] (John 14:27, KJV).

My experience with the old house was my initial lesson in learning to read the fine print and to understand that all His dealings with me are to teach me that He is enough.

⚜ PERSONAL THOUGHTS AND REFLECTIONS

Wait silently before the Lord and ask Him to quiet your heart as you reflect on the truths of this chapter. Before you begin, you might want to pray over and memorize Psalm 142:5: "Then I pray to you, O LORD. I say, 'You are my place of refuge. You are all I really want in life.'"

7. What special insights or Scriptures about God as your Shepherd impressed you?

8. Write down your thoughts concerning why the Lord is committed to meeting your real needs as opposed to meeting your idea of what you think you need.

9. God desires to provide for *all* of our needs: physical, emotional, and spiritual. In which area are you inclined to depend on yourself to have your needs met? In what way can you begin to yield this part of your life to the Lord?

10. How do you sense the Lord is speaking to you about trusting Him as your Shepherd?

11. What is a concrete step you can take to depend on the Lord to be your Shepherd?

12. "When I think of all this, I fall to my knees and pray to the Father" (Ephesians 3:14). Thank God for His gracious heart to shepherd you. Praise Him for His gift of eternal life and for His desire to bestow eternal, not just temporal, gifts upon you. Ask Him to correct and purify your desires. Give thanks that He is Infinite Wisdom and Goodness and that He meets your true needs for your good and for your protection. Ask God to make you aware of anything that hinders your coming to the place He wants to bring you—the place where He satisfies all

your needs. Pray that your trust will grow and that, with joy, you will walk uprightly as you follow and entrust your life to your all-sufficient Shepherd.

"The Lord is my shepherd" . . . *There is a noble tone of confidence about this sentence. There is no "if" nor "but," nor even "I hope so;" but he says, "The Lord is my shepherd." We must cultivate the spirit of assured dependence upon our heavenly Father. The sweetest word of the whole is that monosyllable, "My."*[12]   CHARLES H. SPURGEON

 SCRIPTURE MEMORY

PSALM 23:1—*The LORD is my shepherd; I have all that I need.*

CHAPTER 3

GOD, WHO IS FOR US AND NOT AGAINST US

If God is for us, who can ever be against us?
ROMANS 8:31

*In general, he [Paul] here makes a challenge, throws down the gauntlet,
as it were, dares all the enemies of the saints to do their worst: If God
be for us, who can be against us? The ground of the challenge is God's
being for us; in this he sums up all our privileges. This includes all, that
God is for us; not only reconciled to us, and so not against us, but in
covenant with us, and so engaged for us—all his attributes for us, his
promises for us. All that he is, and has, and does, is for his people.*
MATTHEW HENRY, *Matthew Henry's Commentary on the Whole Bible*

WHAT AN INCREDIBLE CHALLENGE AND what a comforting truth—one that deserves our study and meditation. Warren Wiersbe gives insight to this verse by calling attention to the ministry of our triune God: "*The Father* is for us and proved it by giving His Son (Romans 8:32). *The Son* is for us (Romans 8:34) and so is *the Spirit* (Romans 8:26). God is making all things work for us (Romans 8:28). In His person and His providence, God is for us."[1] In the previous chapter we focused on the Lord as our Shepherd. Now we need to be reminded of just how multifaceted and effective God is in fulfilling His commitment to us. Paul literally forces the issue with his provocative question, "So, what do you think? With

God on our side like this, how can we lose?" (Romans 8:31, MSG). In order to know what we think, it is imperative that we probe the depths of God—the fullness of His being in understanding how very much He is for us and how very much He is *not* against us.

GOD IS FOR US IN HIS FULLNESS

1. "Crucial to the biblical doctrine of God is his Trinitarian nature. Although the term *trinity* is not a biblical word as such, Christian theology has used it to designate the threefold manifestation of the one God as Father, Son, and Holy Spirit. The formulated doctrine of the Trinity asserts the truth that God is one in being or essence who exists eternally in three distinct coequal 'persons.'"[2] How do the following verses confirm the oneness and unity of the ministry of the Trinity?

GENESIS 1:26 ....

EPHESIANS 3:14-19 ....

EPHESIANS 4:4-6 ....

Can we understand the doctrine of the Trinity? We should be warned by the errors that have been made in the past. They have all come about through attempts to simplify the doctrine of the Trinity and make it completely understandable, removing all mystery from it. This we can never do. However, it is not correct to say that we cannot understand the doctrine of the Trinity at all. Certainly we can understand and know that God is three persons, and that each person is fully God, and that there is one God. We can know these things because the Bible teaches them. . . . But what we cannot understand fully is how to fit together those distinct biblical teachings. We wonder how there can be three distinct persons, and each person have the whole being of God in himself, and yet God is only one undivided being. This we are unable to understand. In fact, it is spiritually healthy for us to acknowledge openly that God's very being is far greater than we can ever comprehend. This humbles us before God and draws us to worship him without reservation.[3] WAYNE GRUDEM

2. Identifying the specific roles of each person of the Trinity is beneficial in understanding exactly how God is for us and how

He can be enough for us. Study the passages given below for each one of the Godhead and record the unique and personal manifestations of the Trinity.

a. God the Father: "Over against any abstract neutral meta-physical concept, the God of Scripture is first and foremost a personal being. He reveals himself by names, especially the great personal name Yahweh, 'I AM WHO I AM' (Isaiah 42:8)."[4]

ISAIAH 48:12-13 ....

ISAIAH 57:15 ....

JOHN 3:16 ....

b. Jesus the Christ: "The truth is that the Man who walked among us was a demonstration, not of unveiled deity but of perfect humanity."[5]

ISAIAH 9:6 ···

JOHN 1:1-4 ···

1 TIMOTHY 2:5-6 ···

HEBREWS 7:24-25 ··

c. The Holy Spirit: "The Holy Spirit is the One Who
    makes real in you all that Jesus did for you."[6]

JOHN 3:5-6 ···

JOHN 14:16-17 ··

JOHN 16:7, 13-15 ·· ⌒

GALATIANS 5:22-23 ··· ⌒

─────────── ⌒ ───────────

Nothing can meet our need better than the adoring worship of the Holy Trinity. It is upon God the Father, who has blessed us in Christ Jesus that our expectations rest. It is in Christ that blessing is to be found if we continue close and unceasing fellowship with Him. It is through the Holy Spirit that the presence of the Father and the Son in divine power can be known and experienced.[7]　ANDREW MURRAY

3. Paul ended his letter to the Corinthian church by writing, "May the grace of the Lord Jesus Christ, the love of God, and fellowship of the Holy Spirit be with you all" (2 Corinthians 13:14). Review the verses you have studied in this chapter's previous questions and write down the multiple ways our triune God proves that He is for us.

*On the cross, in agony, he [Jesus] cried out the question,
"Why!?" Why was he being forsaken? (Matthew 27:45-46).
Why was it all necessary? The answer of the Bible is—for us.*[8]

TIMOTHY KELLER

GOD IS FOR US IN OUR TRIALS

4.   Warren Wiersbe called attention to the work of the Trinity in
Romans 8. Carefully read Romans 8:26-39 and recount all the
reasons you can find to answer Paul's challenge of "If God is
for us, who can ever be against us?"

5.   Paul concluded his discourse on the sufficiency of God by
proclaiming that nothing can separate us from God's love and
care. As you study these verses, record the blessings that are
ours because the Lord is for us.

PSALM 16:7-8 ······································

PSALM 56:8-11 ·····································

PSALM 118:5-9 ···································

---

*The believer needs to enter into each new day realizing that
God is for him. There is no need to fear, for his loving Father
desires only the best for His children, even if they must go
through trials to receive His best.*[9]　WARREN WIERSBE

SCRIPTURAL RESPONSES TO GOD'S SUFFICIENCY

When God Didn't Seem to Be Enough

MIRIAM AND AARON

*While they were at Hazeroth, Miriam and Aaron criticized Moses
because he had married a Cushite woman. They said, "Has the
LORD spoken only through Moses? Hasn't he spoken through us,
too?" . . . Then the LORD descended in the pillar of cloud and
stood at the entrance of the Tabernacle. "Aaron and Miriam!" he
called, and they stepped forward. And the LORD said to them,
"Now listen to what I say: If there were prophets among you, I, the
LORD, would reveal myself in visions. I would speak to them in
dreams. But not with my servant Moses. Of all my house, he is the
one I trust. I speak to him face to face, clearly, and not in riddles!
He sees the LORD as he is. So why were you not afraid to criticize
my servant Moses?" The LORD was very angry with them, and he*

departed. As the cloud moved from above the Tabernacle, there
stood Miriam, her skin as white as snow from leprosy.

NUMBERS 12:1-2, 5-10

When God Was Enough

DANIEL

Daniel was a high official during King Darius's reign in Babylon.
Because of Daniel's great ability, the other officials became jealous
and tricked the king into signing a law that targeted Daniel's worship of God. The penalty for praying to anyone except the king
was death by being thrown into the lions' den. The administrators reported that Daniel prayed to his God three times a day and
therefore was guilty of violating the law. Although the king had
high regard for Daniel, he could not protect him from the consequences of his transgression.

> *So at last the king gave orders for Daniel to be arrested and*
> *thrown into the den of lions. The king said to him, "May your*
> *God, whom you serve so faithfully, rescue you." A stone was*
> *brought and placed over the mouth of the den. The king sealed the*
> *stone with his own royal seal and the seals of his nobles, so that*
> *no one could rescue Daniel. . . . Very early the next morning, the*
> *king got up and hurried out to the lions' den. When he got there,*
> *he called out in anguish, "Daniel, servant of the living God! Was*
> *your God, whom you serve so faithfully, able to rescue you from*
> *the lions?" Daniel answered, "Long live the king! My God sent his*
> *angel to shut the lions' mouths so that they would not hurt me, for*
> *I have been found innocent in his sight.*

DANIEL 6:16-17, 19-22

6. Psalm 62:7 states, "My victory and honor come from God alone. He is my refuge, a rock where no enemy can reach me." This verse was certainly true for Moses and Daniel. Express your thoughts about why Miriam, Aaron, and the Babylonian officials would challenge their leaders. What can you learn from these examples about trusting God to be enough for you?

THOUGHTS AND REFLECTIONS
FROM AN OLDER WOMAN

God demonstrates His love for us not by explaining His ways, but by giving us Himself in His fullness. Paul confirmed this truth in Romans 8. He delineated the triune God's great work on our behalf: interceding for us, working all things together for good, sacrificing His own Son, giving us right standing with Himself, and bestowing upon us overwhelming victory that assures us that nothing can defeat or separate us from the love of God. Paul wanted us to be convinced that no matter what our circumstances might be, God is for us.

Paul knew that after making the bold claim of God being for us, he must address the inevitable suffering in life. He confronted this problem by asking another radical question: "Does it mean he no longer loves us if we have trouble or calamity?" (Romans 8:35). Can God really be for us when we experience affliction, pain, and death?

Philip Yancey tackled this issue by stating,

The cross that held Jesus' body, naked and marked
with scars, exposed all the violence and injustice of the
world. At once, the Cross revealed what kind of world
we have and what kind of God we have: a world of gross
unfairness, a God of sacrificial love. No one is exempt
from tragedy or disappointment—God himself was not
exempt. Jesus offered no immunity, no way *out* of the
unfairness, but rather a way *through* it to the other side.
Just as Good Friday demolished the instinctive belief that
this life is supposed to be fair, Easter Sunday followed
with its startling clue to the riddle of the universe. Out
of the darkness, a bright light shone. . . . Someday, God
will restore all physical reality to its proper place under his
reign. Until then, it is a good thing to remember that we
live out our days on Easter Sunday.[10]

The psalmists declared the certainty of God's presence with
them, but they did so in the context of distress, fear of people,
and their assurance of not being shaken. We cannot live with this
certainty unless we believe that God is for us. Comprehending
in some measure the Trinity helps in our belief that surely God
the Father, God the Son, and God the Holy Spirit are committed, in all their fullness, to acting on our behalf. We are created,
redeemed, and indwelt by the living God. "God can do anything,
you know—far more than you could ever imagine or guess or
request in your wildest dreams! He does it not by pushing us
around but by working within us, his Spirit deeply and gently

within us" (Ephesians 3:20, MSG). What more can God do to convince us that He is for us? "For Christ Jesus died *for* us and was raised to life *for* us, and he is sitting in the place of honor at God's right hand, pleading *for* us" (Romans 8:34, emphasis added).

Being confident in God's plan and love is essential in moving through any trials we experience. My living in the old house for four years was an introductory "course" God had for me to learn that He is enough and that His ways (whatever form they may take) are for my ultimate good. God wanted to teach me that it is best to judge my circumstances in light of the Cross. He needed me to know that His presence and work in my life surpass any temporary trial I might have to endure. His purpose was to train me to live out each of my days of disappointment, joy, or trials on Easter Sunday. If the Cross and Resurrection are not enough to prove that God is for me, perhaps I ask too much.

 PERSONAL THOUGHTS AND REFLECTIONS

As you begin, you might want to pray over Psalm 94:14-19. After a period of quieting your heart before the Lord, respond to the following questions.

7. Take time to carefully review this chapter. Write down any new or encouraging thoughts you discovered about God.

8. How does studying the Trinity help you in knowing that God is for you?

9. The New Living Translation refers to God frequently as "The LORD of Heaven's Armies." (Psalm 46:7: "The LORD of Heaven's Armies is here among us; the God of Israel is our fortress.") How does knowing that "The LORD of Heaven's Armies" is for you motivate you to persevere in the midst of troubles and hardships?

10. What problems or hindrances keep you from fully believing that God is for you?

11. What course of action do you need to take in order to embrace the truth that God is for you and not against you?

12. As you close this time of reflection, contemplate this charge from Andrew Murray: "Child of God, bow in deep humility before this blessed Lord Jesus, and worship Him: my Lord and my God! Take time until you come under the full consciousness of an assured faith that as the almighty God, Christ will work for you and in you and through you all that God desires and all that you can need."[11]

To have found God, to have experienced Him in the intimacy of our beings, to have lived even for one hour in the fire of His Trinity and the bliss of His unity clearly makes us say: "Now I understand. You alone are enough for me."[12]

CARLO CORRETTO

 SCRIPTURE MEMORY

ROMANS 8:31—*If God is for us, who can ever be against us?*

God is Enough

CHAPTER 4

SEEKING SATISFACTION IN IDOLS

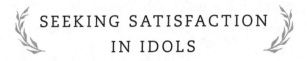

Dear children, keep away from anything that might take God's place in your hearts.

I JOHN 5:21

What is an idol? It is anything more important to you than God, anything that absorbs your heart and imagination more than God, anything you seek to give you what only God can give you.

TIMOTHY KELLER, *Counterfeit Gods*

THE APOSTLE JOHN WAS LIVING in Ephesus when he wrote the epistles we call 1, 2, and 3 John. The chief goddess of the city was Diana. It took two hundred years to complete her temple, which was 420 feet long and 220 feet wide. In the center stood a statue of Diana wrapped in a veil of Persian silk. People came from all over the world to worship her.[1] It was in this context that John ended his letter to the churches of Asia with this solemn command: "Little children, keep yourselves from idols" (1 John 5:21, ESV).

This warning is as applicable to our culture as it was to John's. We are surrounded by a multitude of "Dianas" vying to take God's place in our hearts. John's admonition was to Christians, and because we are vulnerable to "tasting the fruit" of the world, it is our responsibility to keep away from idols—anything that we value and worship more than the Lord—whether it be people, things, or knowledge. Like Eve, our tendency is to be easy prey for something new, something exciting to fill our perceived emptiness. We are consumers to the core, and we seek not only novelty but also fresh, contemporary spiritual experiences. Early church father Augustine was right when he observed that we are restless until we find our rest in God.[2] Therefore, we will explore in this chapter the importance of being diligent in keeping ourselves from anything that might take God's place in our hearts.

☙ THE INSUFFICIENCY OF IDOLS

1. God describes Himself as a jealous God who will not tolerate affection for any other gods (Exodus 20:5). The jealousy that God exhibits is not what we immediately think of as jealousy; He is neither envious nor resentful.

    a. Refer to a dictionary to find the best definition or words that depict God's jealousy.

    b. What do the following verses teach about idol worship and God's jealousy?

EXODUS 20:1-6 ···

EXODUS 34:12-14 ···

JEREMIAH 10:8-11 ···

He is not "jealous," as the Greeks thought, of mere success,
or greatness; but he is very jealous of his own honour, and
will not have the respect and reverence, which is his due,
bestowed on other beings or on inanimate objects.[3]

GEORGE RAWLINSON

2. If anyone could speak about the futility of seeking satisfaction in idols, it would be Solomon. He wrote the book of
Ecclesiastes describing his search for the true meaning of life.
Warren Wiersbe wisely observed, "Solomon had everything,
but his life was empty! There is no need for you and me to
repeat these experiments. Let's accept Solomon's conclusions

and avoid the heartache and pain that must be endured when you experiment in the laboratory of life."[4] Read Ecclesiastes 2. Write down the different ways Solomon attempted to find fulfillment, and record his ultimate conclusion.

--- ⤳ ---

It is our propensity to go off on our own, trying to be human by our own devices and desires, that makes Ecclesiastes necessary reading. Ecclesiastes sweeps our souls clean of all "lifestyle" spiritualties so that we can be ready for God's visitation revealed in Jesus Christ. . . . It is an exposé and rejection of every arrogant and ignorant expectation that we can live by ourselves on our own terms.[5] EUGENE PETERSON

3. In our search for satisfaction, it is easy to allow something good to take God's place in our heart. When we do this, it is idolatry, for anything we love more than God is an idol. Timothy Keller reminds us, "We know a good thing has become a counterfeit god when its demands on you exceed proper boundaries." [6] What potential idols are addressed in the following Scriptures, and in what ways might they "exceed proper boundaries"?

MATTHEW 6:25 ....

LUKE 14:25-27 ···

2 CORINTHIANS 11:3-4 ·······································

COLOSSIANS 2:20-23 ···

---------------------------- & ----------------------------

An idol is whatever you look at and say, in your heart of hearts, "If I have that, then I'll feel my life has meaning, then I'll know I have value, then I'll feel significant and secure."[7]
TIMOTHY KELLER

4. The rich young man had position, possessions, and morality, yet he apparently sensed a need for something more. In the context of our study on idols, what can we learn from the interaction between Jesus and this man (see Mark 10:17-22)?

*Nowhere in the Bible are we taught that a sinner is saved
by selling his goods and giving the money away. . . . Jesus
knew that this man was covetous; he loved material wealth.
By asking him to sell his goods, Jesus was forcing him to
examine his own heart and determine his priorities. With
all of his commendable qualities, the young man still did not
truly love God with all his heart. Possessions were his god.*[8]

WARREN WIERSBE

5. To the Corinthians, Paul wrote, "So, my dear friends, flee from
the worship of idols" (1 Corinthians 10:14). As you reflect on
your study so far, what are some prevalent idols you see in our
world today? What "counterfeit gods" do you think that we,
as believers, especially need to guard against?

*Isn't God enough to meet all your needs, or is His all-
sufficiency too little for your needs? Do you want another
eye beside the one that sees every secret thing? Is His heart
faint? Is His arm weary? If so, seek another god. But if He
is Infinite, Omnipotent, Faithful, True, and All-wise then
why run around looking for another confidence? Why rake*

the earth to find another foundation when this one is strong
enough to bear all the weight you can ever build on?[9]

CHARLES H. SPURGEON

 ## THE SUFFICIENCY OF CHRIST

6. The Lord declared in Isaiah, "Those who still reject me are like
   the restless sea, which is never still but continually churns up
   mud and dirt" (Isaiah 57:20). When you depend on anything
   other than God to fulfill you, you remain restless and empty.
   As you read the Scriptures that follow, record what you learn
   about Christ concerning your inheritance and completeness
   in Him.

GALATIANS 3:24-29

EPHESIANS 1:22-23

COLOSSIANS 2:8-10

The word for "complete" is plēroō. *It means "to be made full." We are filled full in Him. Our fullness comes from His fullness.*[10]

JOHN PHILLIPS

 ## SCRIPTURAL RESPONSES TO GOD'S SUFFICIENCY

When God Didn't Seem to Be Enough

SOLOMON

Solomon started out well as king. He built the temple and prayed a glorious dedication prayer (see 1 Kings 8:22-53). God appeared to him in a dream and granted him wisdom and wealth. God also warned Solomon to obey His decrees and commands. Instead of obedience, though, we find the following account in Scripture:

> *King Solomon loved many foreign women. . . . The LORD had clearly instructed the people of Israel, "You must not marry them, because they will turn your hearts to their gods." Yet Solomon insisted on loving them anyway. He had 700 wives of royal birth and 300 concubines. And in fact, they did turn his heart away from the LORD. In Solomon's old age, they turned his heart to worship other gods instead of being completely faithful to the LORD his God, as his father, David, had been.*
>
> I KINGS 11:1-4

When God Was Enough

SHADRACH, MESHACH, AND ABEDNEGO

Nebuchadnezzar, king of Babylon, made a gold statue ninety feet tall and nine feet wide and commanded everyone to bow down and worship this image whenever certain music was played. The penalty for not bowing down was death in a fiery furnace. Shadrach, Meshach, and Abednego were young Jewish men of noble birth who had been captured by King Nebuchadnezzar, taken to Babylonia, and trained to be administrators. When the music played and everyone else bowed down, these three stood tall. It was reported to the king, who became furious at their insubordination.

> When they were brought in, Nebuchadnezzar said to them, "Is it true, Shadrach, Meshach, and Abednego, that you refuse to serve my gods or to worship the gold statue I have set up? I will give you one more chance to bow down and worship the statue I have made when you hear the sound of the musical instruments. But if you refuse, you will be thrown immediately into the blazing furnace. And then what god will be able to rescue you from my power?" Shadrach, Meshach, and Abednego replied, "O Nebuchadnezzar, we do not need to defend ourselves before you. If we are thrown into the blazing furnace, the God whom we serve is able to save us. He will rescue us from your power, Your Majesty. But even if he doesn't, we want to make it clear to you, Your Majesty, that we will never serve your gods or worship the gold statue you have set up." DANIEL 3:13-18

7. Shadrach, Meshach, and Abednego stand in stark contrast to King Solomon in regard to idol worship. The verse that describes Nebuchadnezzar's astonishment when he sees four men in the fire is a testimony to God's faithfulness and His sufficiency. Nebuchadnezzar shouts, "I see four men, unbound, walking around in the fire unharmed! And the fourth looks like a god!" (Daniel 3:25). After reading these passages, what do you learn from the lives of these men concerning their regard for God and His place in their lives?

THOUGHTS AND REFLECTIONS
FROM AN OLDER WOMAN

As I read God's commands about idols found in Exodus 20, I realize how little I consider His great concern about false gods. False gods are *false*! As we have studied, God is the one true God and He has every right to jealously guard His position in our hearts. The consequences for those who disobey the command "You must not have any other god but me" (Exodus 20:3) are monumental— entire generations are affected. D. Young wrote, "To serve idols, to depend upon anything else than God, anything less than him, anything more easily reached and more easily satisfied—this, when stripped of all disguise, *amounts to hating God*. And a man living in this way is preparing, not only punishments for himself, but miseries for those who come after him."[11] God clearly declared the devastating effects of misplaced affection and dependence. This is why He is rightfully jealous for us: because He knows that He and only He can ever be enough. When we no longer seek or serve idols, then He lavishes unfailing love on a thousand generations.

I think this is why Jesus was so straightforward with the rich young man. It was because Jesus so loved this man that He revealed to him how much he loved his possessions. Keller commented, "Something is safe for us to maintain in our lives only if it has really stopped being an idol. That can happen only when we are truly willing to live without it, when we truly say from the heart, 'Because I have God, I can live without you.'"[12]

First John 5:21 is a simply stated, but powerful, exhortation. *Keep*, in the context of this verse, means to be vigilant, to persist in, to be aware of, and to stay away from anyone or anything that might take God's place in our lives. Only Christ can complete us; we need nothing else. "Since he did not spare even his own Son but gave him up for us all, won't he also give us everything else?" (Romans 8:32). Our satisfaction can only be found in Him. "God is enough" is an incredibly important lesson to learn.

One problem with idols is their subtlety. They can "move" into our hearts without our realizing it. This happened to me a few years ago. A friend sent me a book she thought I would enjoy. The title of the book was *100 Christian Women Who Changed the 20th Century*. There were pictures of very special women on the cover, and I was eager to read about each one. As I opened the book, I noticed that the table of contents was divided into different categories: arts and entertainment, missions, business and politics, literature, Christian ministry and theology, speaking, and marriage and motherhood. All the women listed were gifted teachers, writers, and ministry leaders. I was pleased to add this book to my library.

As I was laying the book down, one other category caught my eye: "Bible Study Ministry." As I read the list of names, I thought, *I write Bible studies, and over the years many women have done my studies, and my name is not there!* Then, *Where did that come from? What was I thinking?* The women in this book were very well-known and mightily used of God. When I had read the book title, it never crossed my mind to think that my name should be included. But now my idol of being noticed, acknowledged, and having prestige rose up and asked me to bow down and give homage. To worship this idol required me to think about poor, left-out me; it caused me to envy, to compare myself to others; it asked me to be ambitious and to seek the spotlight. It made me feel that the best way to be fulfilled was to be honored and recognized. No wonder John wrote, "Little children, keep yourselves from idols" (1 John 5:21, ESV).

I immediately began to pray, and truth flooded my soul: Deny yourself, rejoice when others succeed, have no selfish ambition, seek first the Kingdom of God. And as only God can do, He gently reminded me of the Scripture where the seventy disciples had just returned from their missionary journey with joy and excitement, proclaiming, "Lord, even the demons are subject to us in Your name " (Luke 10:17, NKJV). Jesus acknowledged their given power but concluded His answer to them by stating, *"Do not rejoice in this, that the spirits are subject to you, but rather rejoice because your names are written in heaven"* (Luke 10:20, NKJV, emphasis added).

He, then, whispered in my heart, *Cynthia, your name may not be in that book, but it is in My book, and that is the basis for your joy, and that is all you need.*

All pride is idolatry.[13]   JOHN WESLEY

 PERSONAL THOUGHTS AND REFLECTIONS

As you enter into this time with the Lord, take a few minutes to be silent before Him. Pray over Exodus 34:14: "You must worship no other gods, for the LORD, whose very name is Jealous, is a God who is jealous about his relationship with you." Ask Him to guide your thoughts and responses.

8. Review this chapter and highlight any special thoughts or Scriptures that stood out to you.

9. How has this chapter helped you in understanding the place idols can play in your life?

10. Someone observed, "An idol is anything that, if taken away, you would blame God." What are your thoughts concerning this statement?

11. What is your consuming passion? What is it that you cannot live without? Ask the Lord to pinpoint any "counterfeit gods" you might have.

12. Examine your heart to determine how you might be seeking fulfillment in idols. What can you do to keep away from anything that might take God's place in your heart? Write down your thoughts.

13. Close with prayer, thanking Him that you have been made full and complete in Christ and for the rich and glorious inheritance that is yours. Praise Him that He is Infinite, Omnipotent, Faithful, True, and All-Wise. Pray that you would have spiritual wisdom and insight so that you might grow in your knowledge of God. Ask God to prompt you any time you begin to seek satisfaction in an idol, and resolve that you will become sternly zealous in guarding your heart against all idolatry. Tell Him of your desire to let Him be your all in all and that you desire nothing on earth besides Him.

George Mueller, at more than ninety years of age, in an address to ministers and other Christian workers, said,

I was converted in November 1825, but I didn't come to the point of total surrender of my heart until four years later, in July 1829. It was then I realized my love for money, prominence, position, power, and worldly pleasure was gone. God, and He alone, became my all in all. In Him I found everything I needed, and I desired nothing else.[14]

 ## SCRIPTURE MEMORY

I JOHN 5:21—*Dear children, keep away from anything that might take God's place in your hearts.*

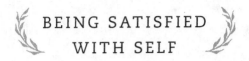 BEING SATISFIED WITH SELF

Love cares more for others than for self. Love doesn't want what it doesn't have. Love doesn't strut, doesn't have a swelled head, doesn't force itself on others, isn't always "me first."

1 CORINTHIANS 13:4-5, MSG

If thou could'st empty all thyself of self,
Like to a shell disinhabited,
Then might He find thee on the ocean shelf,
And say, "This is not dead,"
And fill thee with Himself instead.

But thou art all replete with very thou,
And hast such shrewd activity,
That when He comes He says, "This is enow
Unto itself—'Twere better let it be,
It is so small and full, there is no room for Me."

T. E. BROWNE, *"If Thou Could'st Empty All Thyself of Self"*

WHEN OUR OLDEST DAUGHTER WAS three years old, I asked her to hold my hand as we crossed a busy street. She looked up at me, clasped her hands together, and proclaimed, "I hold my own hand." Out of the mouth of a child came this simple and striking description of pride: holding our own hands.

It is this deceptive self-confidence and independence that keeps us from allowing God to fill us and to be enough. Our tenacious pride drives us to be self-sufficient. We foolishly tell ourselves, "I know what is best," "I can take care of myself," or "If I'm in control, then I can determine what happens." Oswald Chambers minced no words when he defined pride in this way: "Pride is the deification of self."[1]

Chambers also reminded us, "[God] can do nothing for us if we think we are sufficient of ourselves; we have to enter into His Kingdom through the door of destitution. As long as we are rich, possessed of anything in the way of pride or independence, God cannot do anything for us."[2] It is true that when we are full of ourselves (like the shell on the ocean shelf), we have no room for Him in our lives. When we are dependent on our own wisdom and strength, we become our own shepherd and are left holding our own hand.

PRIDE: FULL OF SELF

1. Lawrence Richards wrote, "The pride of the creature who seeks to displace God as the center of the universe and deny the Lord the glory due him may well be the root cause of all the evil that mars the universe and, specifically, of man's original sin (Genesis 3:4-5)."[3] Many scholars, but not all, believe that Isaiah's description of a Babylonian king's arrogant desires, found in Isaiah 14, depicts the fall of Satan from heaven. However we choose to interpret these grand poetic verses, they nevertheless vividly depict the heart of arrogance. Read Isaiah 14:12-14 and summarize the essence of pride.

———————— ℰ ————————

*Pride is Satan's specialty. It is the characteristic that most
aptly describes him. Pride is the issue that had him expelled
from heaven. . . . The most effective means the enemy has to
keep believers from being full of the Spirit is to keep us full of
ourselves.*[4]   BETH MOORE

2. Proverbs teaches that "pride goes before destruction, and
   haughtiness before a fall" (Proverbs 16:18). Study the men in
   the following Scriptures and recount how their pride resulted
   in their destruction.

   NUMBERS 16:1-35 ··································

   DANIEL 5:17-30 • *Daniel was summoned by King Belshazzar to interpret the mysterious writing on the wall.* ··························

3. Naaman, captain of the army of the king of Aram, was stricken
   with leprosy. As you read Naaman's story in 2 Kings 5:1-19,
   describe how God orchestrated people and events to humble
   Naaman and reveal his pride.

Timothy Keller wrote, "Until Naaman learned that God was a God of grace, whose salvation cannot be earned, only received, he would continue to be enslaved to his idols. He would continue to use them to earn a security and significance that they could not produce."[5] Record your thoughts concerning Keller's observations of what Naaman needed to learn about his pride in regard to truly knowing God.

"Just wash yourself," then, was hard because it was so easy. To do it, Naaman had to admit he was helpless and weak and had to receive his salvation as a free gift. It you want God's grace, all you need is need, all you need is nothing. But that kind of spiritual humility is hard to muster. We come to God saying, "Look at all I've done," or maybe "Look at all I've suffered." God, however, wants us to look to him—to just wash. Naaman needed to learn how to "lay his deadly doing down." That phrase comes from an old hymn:

> *Lay your deadly "doing" down*
> *Down at Jesus' feet.*
> *Stand in him, in him alone,*
> *Gloriously complete.*[6]

TIMOTHY KELLER

4. When writing about the Day of the Lord, Isaiah stated, "Human pride will be brought down, and human arrogance will be humbled. Only the LORD will be exalted on that day of judgment" (Isaiah 2:11). What else can you learn about God's response to pride from the following verses?

PSALM 138:6

PROVERBS 16:5

PROVERBS 21:4

5. Jesus gave a realistic portrayal of pride in describing the Pharisees. Record His observations of pride and His teaching on self-promotion found in Matthew 23:1-7 and Luke 14:7-9.

6. The apostle Paul serves as an example of how much God opposes pride in His children. Read 2 Corinthians 12:7-10 and comment on the extent to which God will go to counteract pride and to instill humility.

--- ∞ ---

Pride cannot live beneath the cross.[7]   CHARLES SPURGEON

✺ HUMILITY: EMPTY OF SELF

7. As we lay aside pride, we begin to have a new perspective toward ourselves. Study these verses and record what you learn about how we are to properly view ourselves and live free of pride.

LUKE 9:23 ···

ROMANS 12:3 ···

2 CORINTHIANS 5:15 ....

GALATIANS 6:3-5 ....

———————— ❧ ————————

What then should our attitude be to ourselves? It is a combination of self-affirmation and self-denial—affirming everything in us which comes to us from our creation and redemption, and denying everything which can be traced to the fall.[8]   JOHN STOTT

8. Read 1 Corinthians 13:4-7, where Paul described a life that is no longer filled with self, but with the love of Christ. What can you learn from these verses about how a "pride-free" life should be lived?

———————— ❧ ————————

Young man, the secret of my success is that at an early age I discovered that I was not God.[9]

OLIVER WENDELL HOLMES JR.

SCRIPTURAL RESPONSES TO GOD'S SUFFICIENCY

When God Didn't Seem to Be Enough

THE PHARISEE

Jesus related a parable of two men: one a Pharisee and one a tax
collector.

> *Jesus told this story to some who had great confidence in their own*
> *righteousness and scorned everyone else: "Two men went to the*
> *Temple to pray. One was a Pharisee, and the other was a despised*
> *tax collector. The Pharisee stood by himself and prayed this prayer:*
> *'I thank you, God, that I am not like other people—cheaters,*
> *sinners, adulterers. I'm certainly not like that tax collector! I fast*
> *twice a week, and I give you a tenth of my income.'"*
>
> LUKE 18:9-12

When God Was Enough

THE TAX COLLECTOR

> *The tax collector stood at a distance and dared not even lift his*
> *eyes to heaven as he prayed. Instead, he beat his chest in sorrow,*
> *saying, "O God, be merciful to me, for I am a sinner." I tell you,*
> *this sinner, not the Pharisee, returned home justified before God.*
> *For those who exalt themselves will be humbled, and those who*
> *humble themselves will be exalted.* LUKE 18:13-14

9. As you reflect on these passages, describe the mind-set of the
   prideful Pharisee and the attitude of the humble tax collector.
   In what way does this parable speak to you?

The beginning of all prayer, Christ reminds us, is the taking of the sinner's place, and the simple appeal for mercy. And as it is the first, so it is the cry ever pulsing through prayer. It is never wanting from the justified. The pardon has been received. The blood cleanses from all sin; but not the less, but all the more, is the knowledge of sin and the need of the ever-renewed application of mercy. This is humility—sinful self cast on Divine mercy, and, forgiven much, loving much. There is no measurement with other men, for God is all in all.[10]

J. MARSHALL LANG

THOUGHTS AND REFLECTIONS FROM AN OLDER WOMAN

I was honored to be asked to speak again at a church in Ohio. Although several years had passed, I was looking forward to staying in the same home and renewing my acquaintance with this lovely family. On this trip my dear friend Danna accompanied me. We were picked up at the airport by our hostess and driven to her home. After getting settled, we congregated in the kitchen to visit and help with dinner. The table was already set, and I noticed a red "You Are Special" plate among the place settings. This brought back memories, because at my first visit, I was given this significant plate. The table was in the large kitchen, and as the time to be seated drew near, I started to put my water glass at the "red plate" setting. I was thinking, *I am the speaker for the weekend, and on my previous visit I was given this special plate, so I'm sure that this is my place.* I was momentarily distracted during the last-minute preparations, and before I could claim this "seat of honor," our hostess announced, "Danna, in our family we have a tradition of honoring our first-time guests with the special red plate, so please sit here. This is our way of welcoming you into our home."

Oh, my! Immediately I was reminded of Jesus' teaching on humility: "When you are invited to a wedding feast, don't sit in the seat of honor. What if someone who is more distinguished than you has also been invited? The host will come and say, 'Give this person your seat.' Then you will be embarrassed, and you will have to take whatever seat is left at the foot of the table!" (Luke 14:8-9). With a grateful heart I prayed, *Oh, Lord, thank You for sparing me from being asked to move to the foot of the table. How prideful and presumptuous of me to think that the red plate was for me.*

Andrew Murray rightly observed, "'Me' is a most exacting person, requiring the best seat and the highest place for itself, and feeling grievously wounded if its claim is not recognized."[11]

C. S. Lewis described pride in this way: "Pride is spiritual cancer; it eats up the very possibility of love, or contentment, or even common sense."[12] Pride is indeed a spiritual cancer. Pride consumes love because pride cares more for self than for others. The Pharisee's only notice of the tax collector was to acknowledge his superiority. Chambers warned, "Beware of anything that puts you in the superior person's place."[13]

Pride eats up contentment. I am convicted every time I read Moses' words spoken to Korah:

Now listen, Levites! *Isn't it enough* for you that the God of Israel has separated you from the Israelite community to bring you near to Himself, to perform the work at the LORD's tabernacle, and to stand before the community to minister to them? He has brought you near, and all your fellow Levites who are with you, but you are seeking the priesthood as well.

NUMBERS 16:8-10, HCSB, EMPHASIS ADDED

Pride continues to demand more—more recognition and more control. We cannot be content because pride is always seeking for the "best seat and highest place."

Pride eats up common sense. My common sense was devoured when I assumed that the special plate was for me. If I had relinquished my *me first* attitude, perhaps my common sense would have kicked in and I would have discerned who the plate was for, or at least not have made such a prideful supposition.

Leprosy in biblical times can be compared to cancer in our day. Although Naaman had status, wealth, and power, he was literally being "eaten up" by his disease. He thought that his position and affluence could procure his physical healing, and he was pridefully confident in his ability to get what he needed.

Naaman learned, though, that he could not control his life or manipulate circumstances the way he wanted. He learned that he was not sufficient in himself. In order to receive wholeness, he had to enter through the door of destitution. He had to lay his "deadly doing down" and humble himself under the mighty hand of God. He would agree with King Nebuchadnezzar: "I . . . praise and glorify and honor the King of heaven. All his acts are just and true, and he is able to humble the proud" (Daniel 4:37).

This is good news. God is able to deal with our pride—Paul and Naaman are prime examples. We find healing for our leprosy by recognizing our poverty and insufficiency to live in our own strength. It is taking ourselves off the throne of our hearts and enthroning the Lord Jesus Christ; it is turning from our selfish ways, taking up our cross daily, and following Him (Luke 9:23). It is accepting the only cure for the cancer of pride: Jesus' death and sacrifice on the cross on our behalf.

My closing signature in every e-mail and letter I write is "Keep your hand in His." It is a constant reminder of my dependence on the Lord and is the best way to keep from holding my own hand.

PERSONAL THOUGHTS AND REFLECTIONS

After quieting your heart, pray over Paul's testimony to the church in Corinth: "We have depended on God's grace, not on our own human wisdom" (2 Corinthians 1:12). Assure the Lord that you desire His wisdom as you answer the following questions:

10. Review this chapter and summarize your key thoughts concerning pride.

11. What particular passage helped you to acknowledge your *me first* attitude?

12. In what areas are you most tempted to compare yourself to others or to hold your own hand?

13. Ask the Lord to point out any blind spots you might have in recognizing pride in your own life. Pray for wisdom in learning how to empty yourself in order to be filled with Christ.

14. Have you opened the door of destitution and accepted God's free gift of salvation? We learn from Naaman that God is a God of grace, and there is nothing you can do in and of yourself to earn or merit His love and forgiveness. If it is your desire to accept Christ as your personal Lord and Savior, then humbly admit that you are a sinner in need of forgiveness. Confess your belief that Jesus Christ died on the cross for your sins and express your desire to love and follow Him. "Since we believe that Christ died for all, we also believe that we have all died to our old life. He died for everyone so that those who receive his new life will no longer live for themselves. Instead, they will live for Christ, who died and was raised for them" (2 Corinthians 5:14-15). Record the date you prayed this prayer in your Bible to mark the beginning of your new life in Christ.

15. Close with prayer, humbly entreating God to deliver you from the spiritual cancer of pride. Ask Him to point out the specific ways you exhibit pride. Request that He show you your "shrewd activity"—the deadly doing that you need to lay down in order to be free from self and filled with His Spirit. Pray to have an honest evaluation of yourself. Pray that you can empty "all thyself of self" so that there is abundant room for Him. Ask that as you keep your hand in His, you will reflect Christ's humble and gentle spirit and His love in you will be evident to all. Pray that you will no longer live for yourself but for Christ, willing to love and serve others in humble obedience.

SCRIPTURE MEMORY

1 CORINTHIANS 13:4-5—*Love cares more for others than for self. Love doesn't want what it doesn't have. Love doesn't strut, doesn't have a swelled head, doesn't force itself on others, isn't always "me first." (MSG)*

CHAPTER 6

TAKING OFFENSE

When John heard in prison about the deeds of the Christ, he sent word by his disciples and said to him, "Are you the one who is to come, or shall we look for another?" And Jesus answered them, "Go and tell John what you hear and see: the blind receive their sight and the lame walk, lepers are cleansed and the deaf hear, and the dead are raised up, and the poor have good news preached to them. And blessed is the one who is not offended by me."

MATTHEW 11:2-6, ESV

Blessed is he who is not offended in Christ; who recognizes Christ's spiritual greatness, Christ's infinite goodness, Christ's deep and holy love. Blessed is he who sees nothing in Christ to repel, but everything to attract and to convince. He is blessed, for he will find in Christ all that he needs—peace, comfort, hope, rest for his soul.

B. C. CAFFIN, *The Pulpit Commentary*

JOHN THE BAPTIST, IN PRISON for several months, finally sent his disciples to ask Jesus if He was the Messiah. John had to be restless; he was not used to confinement, and in the darkness and wretchedness of his cell, he had a moment of doubt. He needed assurance that Jesus was the One who would usher in the Kingdom of Heaven. Perhaps John was beginning to think, *Look at all I have done to serve Jesus. I have faithfully prepared the way for the Lord, yet nothing has radically changed. This is not the way it is supposed to be. Jesus has not declared Himself King—maybe He is not the Messiah.*

Doubt
uncertainty

When surrounded by doubt and uncertainty, it becomes easy to take up an offense—to feel slighted or violated—toward someone who has disappointed or hurt us. The bottom line of our disillusionment is ultimately God. We tell ourselves, "I have done everything right and now I have this tragedy to face; God is not fair, other people I know are not suffering like I am; where is the abundant life Jesus promised? This is not what I signed up for; God owes me for all I have done for Him." When we find ourselves imprisoned and disillusioned by overwhelming circumstances, John's question echoes our own—"God, are You really who You say You are? Are You really enough?" Jesus gave a profound answer and we must examine it in order to deal with our unmet expectations and our assumed offenses from God.

❧ TAKING OFFENSE

1. Albert Barnes commented, "The word *offense* means a *stumbling block*. This verse [Matthew 11:6] might be rendered, 'Happy is he to whom I shall not prove a stumbling-block.'"[1] Study these verses and record who and why people were offended.

MATTHEW 13:54-57 ....

MATTHEW 15:1-12 ....

ROMANS 9:30-33 .... ꝏ

2. One of the best illustrations of people who had a "right" to be offended is recounted in Matthew 20:1-16. Read this passage and write down your thoughts about why the landowner responded the way he did.

The landowner felt they should be thankful to have work, but instead were angry that they didn't get paid more than those who didn't work as long

---------------------- ꝏ ----------------------

It never crossed my mind that he [the landowner] might have acted on the supposition that those who had worked in the vineyard the whole day would be deeply grateful to have had the opportunity to do work for their boss, and even more grateful to see what a generous man he was.[2]

HENRI J. M. NOUWEN

3. Jesus told a parable found in Luke 15:11-32; it is the story known as "the prodigal son." It is paradoxical that this parable in itself was offensive to many of the listeners—mainly the Pharisees. Timothy Keller observed, "No, the original listeners were not melted into tears by this story but rather they were thunderstruck, offended, and infuriated. Jesus' purpose is not to warm our hearts but to shatter our categories. Through this

parable Jesus challenges what nearly everyone has ever thought about God, sin, and salvation."[3] Carefully read this parable and answer the following questions.

What was the younger son's perceived offense toward his father? Please describe.

disrespect, betrayal

What godly qualities did the father demonstrate toward his young son before the son left and after he returned?

Forgiveness, Love, acceptance

———— ❧ ————

When Luke writes, "and left for a distant country," he indicates much more than the desire of a young man to see more of the world. He speaks about a drastic cutting loose from the way of living, thinking, and acting that has been handed down to him from generation to generation as a sacred legacy. More than disrespect, it is a betrayal of the treasured values of family and community. The "distant country" is the world in which everything considered holy at home is disregarded.[4]   HENRI J. M. NOUWEN

In what way did the father attempt to reassure and encourage his elder son?

How did the older brother express his offense toward his father?

Pride in his good deeds, rather than remorse over his bad deeds, was keeping the older son out of the feast of salvation. The elder brother's problem is his self-righteousness, the way he uses his moral record to put God and others in his debt to control them and get them to do what he wants.[5]

TIMOTHY KELLER

4. "The word 'prodigal' does not mean 'wayward' but, according to *Merriam-Webster's Collegiate Dictionary*, 'recklessly spendthrift.' It means to spend until you have nothing left. This term is therefore as appropriate for describing the father in the story as his younger son. . . . Jesus is showing us the God of Great Expenditure, who is nothing if not prodigal toward us,

his children."[6] Write a brief summary expressing your thoughts about how this parable portrays God's daring lavishness.

--- ❧ ---

The disposition of sin is not immorality and wrong-doing, but the disposition of self-realization—I am my own god. This disposition may work out in decorous morality or in indecorous immorality, but it has the one basis, my claim to my right to myself.[7]　　OSWALD CHAMBERS

CHOOSING TO TRUST

5. Trust in God's preeminence and His ways can keep us from stumbling. Since we are finite beings, it can be difficult to grasp the infinite. What do these Scriptures teach about how we should regard God in light of our circumstances?

ECCLESIASTES 11:5 ·······························

ISAIAH 40:13-14 ·······························

ISAIAH 55:8-9 ....

ROMANS 11:33-36 ....

—————————— ⟋ ——————————

It does little good for us to object to what He chooses to do.
When He said to Moses, "I AM that I AM" He in effect said
I am Who I am and not Who you would prefer Me to be.[8]

ERWIN W. LUTZER

6. God's ways are not our ways, but they are always right. As you go through the trials of life, you can be confident that God is at work. How do these verses encourage you to trust the Lord during hard times?

JEREMIAH 17:7-8 ....

ROMANS 8:28 ....

7. Read Isaiah 61:1-2 and review Matthew 11:2-6. John the Baptist's request was heartfelt and sincere. In essence, he was asking if Jesus truly was the Messiah. How do you think Jesus' answer gives the assurance that John needed?

―――――――――― ◠◠ ――――――――――

[Jesus] is a king who wants not subservience, but love. Thus, rather than mowing down Jerusalem, Rome, and every other worldly power, he chose the slow, hard way of Incarnation, love, and death. A conquest from within.[9]

PHILIP YANCEY

 SCRIPTURAL RESPONSES TO GOD'S SUFFICIENCY

When God Didn't Seem to Be Enough

MANY OF CHRIST'S DISCIPLES

[Jesus said,] "I live because of the living Father who sent me; in the same way, anyone who feeds on me will live because of me.

*I am the true bread that came down from heaven. Anyone who
eats this bread will not die as your ancestors did (even though they
ate the manna) but will live forever." He said these things while
he was teaching in the synagogue in Capernaum. Many of his
disciples said, "This is very hard to understand. How can anyone
accept it?" Jesus was aware that his disciples were complaining, so
he said to them, "Does this offend you? Then what will you think
if you see the Son of Man ascend to heaven again? The Spirit
alone gives eternal life. Human effort accomplishes nothing. And
the very words I have spoken to you are spirit and life. But some
of you do not believe me.". . . At this point many of his disciples
turned away and deserted him.* JOHN 6:57-64, 66

When God Was Enough

HABAKKUK

*Even though the fig trees have no blossoms, and there are no grapes
on the vines; even though the olive crop fails, and the fields lie
empty and barren; even though the flocks die in the fields, and
the cattle barns are empty, yet I will rejoice in the LORD! I will
be joyful in the God of my salvation! The Sovereign LORD is my
strength! He makes me as surefooted as a deer, able to tread upon
the heights.* HABAKKUK 3:17-19

8. As you reflect on these passages, comment on what prompted
"the many disciples" to turn away and what caused Habakkuk
to respond the way he did.

THOUGHTS AND REFLECTIONS
FROM AN OLDER WOMAN

In the early 1950s, Elisabeth Elliot went to Ecuador as a Bible translator. In her book *These Strange Ashes*, she recounted the story of finding Don Macario, who was the perfect answer to her prayer for someone to help her learn the language and to assist her in translating the Bible into the Colorado language. He was a Christian, completely bilingual, and in need of work.

After they had been working together for a while, she received the tragic news one day that Macario had been murdered over a land dispute. She was shocked at this loss of life and loss of her helper and honestly expressed her doubts.

> As I look back on that time, I think it was Lesson One
> for me in the school of faith. That is, it was my first
> experience of having to bow down before that which
> I could not possibly explain. . . . Faith's most severe
> tests come not when we see nothing, but when we see
> a stunning array of evidence that seems to prove our
> faith vain. If God were God, if He were omnipotent, if
> He had cared, would this have happened? Is this that
> I face now the ratification of my calling, the reward of
> obedience? . . . I had desired God Himself and He had
> not only not given me what I asked for, He had snatched
> away what I had.[10]

Elisabeth seemed to echo the thoughts of John the Baptist: "Is this my reward for obedience? Are you truly the One?"

How did Elisabeth reconcile the fact that the God she loved

and served was also the God who was not always who she preferred Him to be? Here are her thoughts:

> It was a long time before I came to the realization that it is in our acceptance of what is given that God gives Himself. . . . Each separate experience of individual stripping we may learn to accept as a fragment of the suffering Christ bore when He took it all. "Surely he hath borne our griefs and carried our sorrows." This grief, this sorrow, this total loss that empties my hands and breaks my heart, I may, if I will, accept, and by accepting it, I find in my hands something to offer. And so I give it back to Him who in mysterious exchange gives Himself to me.[11]

Trusting God as the great I AM is at the heart of not doubting Him. We are vulnerable to the whispers of the enemy, who tells us that God is not fair, that if He were a God of love, this tragedy would not have happened. Certainly His silence is evidence of His absence and lack of concern for what we are going through.

Elisabeth experienced what Oswald Chambers calls "the discipline of dismay." Chambers explains, "The discipline of dismay is essential in the life of discipleship. . . . When the darkness of dismay comes, endure until it is over, because out of it will come that following of Jesus which is an unspeakable joy."[12] Grasping the truth of God's love and sacrifice, His ultimate desire to give Himself, and His just and righteous ways keeps us from being offended. It also involves understanding that the discipline of dismay is an intrinsic part in the life of a disciple—in a mysterious way, as we endure, God gives us Himself and proves that He is enough.

Randy Alcorn made this observation:

Some people can't believe God would create a world in which people would suffer so much. Isn't it more remarkable that God would create a world in which no one would suffer more than he? God's Son bore no guilt of his own; he bore ours. In his love for us, God self-imposed the sentence of death on our behalf. One thing we must never say about God—that he doesn't understand what it means to be abandoned utterly, suffer terribly, and die miserably.[13]

John the Baptist gives us an example of what to do when we doubt God. We take our confusion to the Lord and ask for wisdom. We must understand, though, that we may not hear immediately or receive a specific response to our question.

Mike Mason commented on how God responded to Job's questions, saying, "If we find it exasperating that God never gives Job any reasons for his long ordeal of suffering, then we have entirely missed the point of these final chapters. While it is true that the Lord's answer to Job is neither logical nor theological, this is not the same as saying that He gives no answer. The Lord *does* give an answer. His answer is Himself."[14]

Jack and I have a treasured bronze depiction of the prodigal's father rushing out to meet his son. It is entitled "Father's Love." With an expression of pure joy on his face and with outstretched arms, the figure of the father is cast in the act of running to embrace his son. This statue is a graphic and constant reminder of how very much our heavenly Father loves us and of how much He desires for us to trust Him and to believe that He is enough.

PERSONAL THOUGHTS AND REFLECTIONS

Seek to be still before the Lord, and pray over Romans 8:29 from *The Message*: "God knew what he was doing from the very beginning. He decided from the outset to shape the lives of those who love him along the same lines as the life of his Son." Pray for God to guide you as you consider your answers to the following thoughts.

9. As you reviewed this chapter, what truth or Scriptures spoke to you? God's ways are not our ways, but they are always right. God is at work - trust the Lord during hard times

10. What did you learn about God's love and character in the passages you studied? God created a world in which no one would suffer more than Him.
unconditional - just & Holy

11. How does comprehending the greatness of God's wisdom and ways help you in trusting Him? Trusting God as the Great "I Am" is at the heart of not doubting Him.

12. Ask God to search your heart for times when He was not the God you would prefer for Him to be. Pray over these
their is no sin too big to forgive.

circumstances, acknowledge His sovereignty, and renew your trust in His infinite goodness.

When asking God to change a friend & soften her heart, and change my attitude

13. From the Scriptures you studied, write two or three sentences summarizing how you know that "God is enough."

14. As you pray, ask God to search your heart for any unconfessed offenses you have against Him. Run to Him in repentance. Share your heart concerning your doubts and wounds. Tell the Lord that you desire to trust His ways and to learn acceptance and endurance as His disciple. Ask for increased faith in His plan and provision for you. Thank Him that He understands and has experienced the discipline of dismay in a far greater way than you can imagine or comprehend. Rejoice that His answers to your questions will always include the gift of Himself. Commit your way to His ways and, with great faith, place your hand in His. Close by praying Habakkuk 3:17-19.

In the parable the father says to his son, "My property is thine—thine to use and to enjoy; there is nothing I have made that is within your view and your reach which you are not free to partake of and employ; all that I have is thine." Is not that our goodly estate as the sons of God? This world is God's property, and he shares it with us. He interdicts, indeed, that which would do us harm or do injury to others. Otherwise he says to us, "Take and partake, enrich your hearts with all that is before you." And this applies not only to all material gifts, but to all spiritual good—to knowledge, wisdom, truth, love, goodness; to those great spiritual qualities which are the best and most precious of the Divine possessions.[15]

W. CLARKSON

 SCRIPTURE MEMORY

MATTHEW 11:6—*Blessed is the one who is not offended by me. (ESV)*

 HAVING LITTLE FAITH

Jesus responded, "Why are you afraid? You have so little faith!"
MATTHEW 8:26

True faith depends not at all upon itself, nor upon its own system of piety, but rather upon the Lord alone and His faithfulness. It knows that our faith in God is only a reflection of God's faith in us . . . To have faith is to have trust in the faithfulness of our God, knowing that faithfulness is first and foremost not a human but a divine attribute.
MIKE MASON, *The Gospel According to Job*

AFTER A FULL DAY OF ministry, Jesus and His disciples were crossing the Sea of Galilee when a sudden, violent storm battered the boat with such high waves that the disciples feared for their lives. Terrified, they shouted to Jesus, who was asleep, " 'Lord, save us! We're going to drown!' Jesus responded, 'Why are you afraid? You have so little faith!' Then he got up and rebuked the wind and waves, and suddenly there was a great calm. The disciples were amazed. 'Who is this man?' they asked. 'Even the winds and waves obey him'" (Matthew 8:23-27). B. C. Caffin answers the disciples' question in this way: " 'What manner of man is this?' All things obey him: the storms of nature and the storms of the restless heart. 'What manner of man is this?' The Man of Sorrows; the Word made flesh; the Son of God, 'who loved me, and gave himself for me.'"[1]

We have studied the commitment of the Godhead on our behalf. We have been assured that God is our Shepherd and that He is for us, but often we encounter storms where we feel that we are battling the waves alone. The disciples, feeling alone and fearing for their lives, cried out to the Lord in desperation. Matthew Henry commented, "He does not chide them for disturbing him with their prayers, but for disturbing themselves with their fears."[2] It is time to examine our "little" faith in regard to how we respond to the difficulties and pain of life. The reason that the disciples were amazed was that only God, who created the wind and the waves, could command them to be still. It is our powerful and sovereign God who is with us—need we ever doubt or be afraid?

❦ OUR NEED FOR GOD'S FAITHFULNESS

1. When assailed by affliction, we can recall God's mercy and grace poured out on us while we were still sinners. "God showed his great love for us by sending Christ to die for us while we were still sinners" (Romans 5:8). In what ways do the following passages help you to understand the love and sacrifice that "*faithed*" us into existence?

ROMANS 4:5-8 ....

God justifies the unGodLy — Our sins & transgressions are forgiven and the Lord will never count those sins Against us

ROMANS 8:1-2 ....

Through Christ Jesus we are set free from the Law of Sin & Death & Condemnation

EPHESIANS 2:4-5 ....

It is by Gods Grace & mercy that We have been Saved, (In spite of Ourselfs + Sin)

1 PETER 1:18-21 ....

Our Salvation is from the Sacrafice of Jesus christ, (not because by riches or Gold) (or Ancestors)

Your confidence in the love nature of God is crucial. This has been a powerful influence in my life. I always view my circumstances against the backdrop of the cross, where God clearly demonstrated once and for all His deep love for me. I may not always understand my current situation or how things will eventually turn out, but I can trust in the love Christ proved to me when He laid down His life for me on the cross. In the death and resurrection of Jesus Christ, God forever convinced me that He loves me. I choose to base my trust in God on what I know—His love for me—and I choose to trust that in time He will help me understand the confusing circumstances I may be experiencing.[3]

HENRY BLACKABY AND RICHARD BLACKABY

2. The psalmist David clearly declared the Lord's personal safe-keeping: "The LORD is my rock, my fortress, and my savior; my God is my rock, in whom I find protection. He is my shield, the power that saves me, and my place of safety" (Psalm 18:2). How do these verses strengthen your faith and calm your fears?

PSALM 27:1-3

The Lord is my strength
and salvation,
I will not fear as my
trust is in the Lord.

ISAIAH 41:10

Don't be fearful or
discouraged – God will
strengthen and help us
uphold

MATTHEW 10:28-31

Do not be afraid

JOHN 14:27

We have Peace in our hearts,
Do not be afraid,
Do not let our hearts
be troubled

Hold on to the faithfulness of God. Believe, when you do not understand, that he knows all about you, that he is committed to taking care of you. He has promised it.[4]

D. MARTYN LLOYD-JONES

3. In commenting on Shadrach, Meshach, and Abednego being thrown into the fiery furnace, Charles Spurgeon wrote, "As sure as God puts His children in the furnace He will be in the furnace with them."[5] Spurgeon calls attention to the fact that God was also in the furnace. Isaiah validated God's presence with us by writing, "Behold, the young woman who is unmarried and a virgin shall conceive and bear a son, and shall call his name Immanuel [God with us]" (Isaiah 7:14, AMPCE). It is essential to remember that in our trials our Immanuel is with us. What encouragement concerning this truth do you receive from these Scriptures?

DEUTERONOMY 31:8

the Lord goes before you and will be with you, he will not leave or forsake us — do not be afraid or discouraged

ISAIAH 43:1-2

no matter what we are dealing with or going through — God is by our side, Do not fear

HEBREWS 13:5-6 ·· ∾

Be Content with what we have
THe Lord is my helper, I
will not be afraid

4. Mike Mason reminds us that our faith depends upon the Lord alone and His faithfulness. How does knowing the Lord's devoted guardianship of you increase your faith and relieve your fears?

I have peace, no anxiety,
no fear because I
know God has a plan
for me. His timing is perfect

Faith in the Bible is faith in God against everything that contradicts Him—I will remain true to God's character whatever He may do. "Though He slay me, yet will I trust Him"—this is the most sublime utterance of faith in the whole of the Bible.[6]
OSWALD CHAMBERS

5. Although the Lord admonishes the disciples for their little faith, He uses the minute mustard seed to teach about faith and the Kingdom of God in the Scriptures below. What can you learn from the mustard seed in regard to having a real and effective faith?

MARK 4:30-32 ·· ∾

a tiny seed planted can
grow into something big —

LUKE 17:5-6 ....

Faith as Small as a mustard seed can grow

This truth is surely not that the possession of a faith as slight *as the mustard seed is small will suffice,* but *that the faith which is* full *as is the mustard seed* of life and power of appropriation *will avail for all occasions. For it is not true that a slight and feeble faith does suffice. . . . Only a faith which is a living and a growing power, like the mustard seed in the soil, will triumph over the difficulties to be met and mastered. . . . It will uproot great evils in God's Name and strength. It will upraise noble structures of good, when inspired at the same source.*[7]   W. CLARKSON

6. "Keep a firm grip on the faith. The suffering won't last forever. It won't be long before this generous God who has great plans for us in Christ—eternal and glorious plans they are!—will have you put together and on your feet for good. He gets the last word; yes, he does" (1 Peter 5:10, MSG). Holding on to our faith is essential for enduring hardship. What do you learn from the following Scriptures about the perspective we should have toward suffering and trials?

JOHN 16:33 ....

We will have challenges and problems, but can have peace because God has overcome the world

ROMANS 8:18 ....

We are Gods children
Our Sufferings Dont Compare
to the Glory that awaits us

2 CORINTHIANS 4:16-18 ....

Do not lose heart,
Dont Dwell on what is now,
but what is eternal.

1 PETER 1:3-7 ....

Throug Gods mercy he
has given us a Living Hope
and an inheritance in
heaven that can never perish

We are bidden to "put on Christ," to become like God.
[Romans 13:14] That is, whether we like it or not, God
intends to give us what we need, not what we now think
we want. Once more, we are embarrassed by the intolerable
compliment, by too much love, not too little.[8]   C. S. LEWIS

7. Paul stated with certainty that God's ways are woven together
    for our good. In Romans he wrote, "That's why we can be so
    sure that every detail in our lives of love for God is worked into
    something good. God knew what he was doing from the very
    beginning. He decided from the outset to shape the lives of
    ~~~e who love him along the same lines as the life of his Son"
    ~~ans 8:28-29, MSG). As you study these passages, what do

you discover about God's purpose for us, and what assurance is given that He works for our good?

JEREMIAH 29:11 ....

He has a plan for us . . . to prosper and not harm, give Hope & have a future

2 CORINTHIANS 3:16-18 ....

In the spirit of the Lord, their is freedom, we are transformed

---

Not until history has run its course will we understand how "all things work together for good." Faith means believing in advance what will only make sense in reverse.[9]

PHILIP YANCEY

SCRIPTURAL RESPONSES TO GOD'S SUFFICIENCY

When God Didn't Seem to Be Enough

THOMAS

One of the twelve disciples, Thomas (nicknamed the Twin), was not with the others when Jesus came. They told him, "We have seen the Lord!" But he replied, "I won't believe it unless I see the nail wounds in his hands, put my fingers into them, and place my hand into the wound in his side." Eight days later the disciples were together again, and this time Thomas was with them. The doors were locked; but suddenly, as before, Jesus was standing among them. "Peace be with you," he said. Then he said to Thomas, "Put your finger here, and look at my hands. Put your hand into the wound in my side. Don't be faithless any longer. Believe!" "My Lord and my God!" Thomas exclaimed. Then Jesus told him, "You believe because you have seen me. Blessed are those who believe without seeing me."   JOHN 20:24-29

When God Was Enough

A ROMAN OFFICER

When Jesus returned to Capernaum, a Roman officer came and pleaded with him, "Lord, my young servant lies in bed, paralyzed and in terrible pain." Jesus said, "I will come and heal him." But the officer said, "Lord, I am not worthy to have you come into my home. Just say the word from where you are, and my servant will be healed. I know this because I am under the authority of my superior officers, and I have authority over my soldiers. I only need to say, 'Go,' and they go, or 'Come,' and they come. And if I say to my slaves, 'Do this,' they do it." When Jesus heard this, he was amazed. Turning to those who were following him, he said, "I tell you the truth, I haven't seen faith like this in all Israel!". . . Then Jesus said to the Roman officer, "Go back home. Because you believed, it has happened." And the young servant was healed that same hour.   MATTHEW 8:5-10, 13

8. A. W. Tozer commented, "We rest in *what God is.* I believe that this alone is true faith. Any faith that must be supported

by the evidence of the senses is not real faith."[10] Contrast the faith of Thomas with that of the Roman soldier. With whom do you most identify? Why?

 ## THOUGHTS AND REFLECTIONS FROM AN OLDER WOMAN

What the Lord desires is faith that will dispel fear and doubt. He desires that we trust Him as our Immanuel who sustains us. Yes, God is with us and for us. He is our rock and our protector. He is our Redeemer and Savior and Shepherd. But that does not mean that we always have calm waters. God was with Shadrach, Meshach, and Abednego, but they still had to go into the fiery furnace. God protected Daniel, but he still spent the night in the lions' den. Jesus was with the disciples in the storm, but they still had to endure the terrifying waves. God's grace was sufficient for Paul's thorn in the flesh, but he still had to live with the thorn for the rest of his life. At a conference someone humorously asked me, "Don't you think Christians should get a discount on suffering?"

Elisabeth Elliot's faith was tested with fiery trials and violent storms. After her translation helper was murdered, Elisabeth married Jim Elliot, who had a heart to evangelize the Auca Indians of Ecuador. Jim and four other missionaries were later speared to death while attempting to share Christ with the Aucas. She made this observation after her husband's death: "God is God. That was the stunning lesson of that most stunning event in my life. Jim's death required me to deny God or believe him, to trust him or renounce him. The lesson is the same for all of us. The contexts differ."[11] Elisabeth experienced a horrifying storm, but she ultimately had to answer the questions, "Will you still trust Me? Am I enough for you?" Her answer was yes, for after a period of time and God's providential leading, she chose to live among the Aucas for two years, where she shared the Good News of Christ. The faith that God wanted of Elisabeth and wants of us is that of fully trusting Him while walking through deep rivers of difficulty.

Max Lucado relates a profound experience of learning that "God is God" and the necessity of faith regardless of circumstances. He wrote,

> In *God Came Near* I've told how our oldest daughter fell into a swimming pool when she was two years old. A friend saw her and pulled her to safety. What I didn't tell was what happened the next morning in my prayer time. I made a special effort to record my gratitude in my journal. I told God how wonderful he was for saving her. As clearly as if God himself were speaking, this question came to mind: *Would I be less wonderful had I let her drown? Would I be any less a good God for calling her home? Would I still be receiving your praise this morning had I not saved her? Is God still a good God when he says no?*[12]

Adversity is an ever-present reality here on earth. Jesus taught, "In this godless world you will continue to experience difficulties. But take heart! I've conquered the world" (John 16:33, MSG). In this godless world we will experience difficulties, but God wants us to keep holding on to His hand by faith as He walks with us. He is with us to protect and guard our hearts above all. In 1678 this insightful thought was written: "Though God does not always deliver his people out of trouble, yet he delivers them from the evil of trouble, the despair of trouble, by supporting the spirit."[13]

Certainly the Lord demonstrated His power when He commanded the waves and wind to cease, and the disciples were amazed. We, too, must stand in awe. Who is this man who has conquered the world? He is the Man of Sorrows, the Word made flesh, the Son of God. How we respond to our trials should reflect our faith in who He is. Will we doubt and mistrust Him because we suffer? Will we live in fear and anxiety because we believe that somehow our almighty God might be asleep? The issue is never the storm, the issue is our faith. Oswald Chambers declared, "The great thing about faith in God is that it keeps a man undisturbed in the midst of disturbance."[14]

My dear friend Mary Beth shared this insight about Jesus being asleep during the storm: When we are being overwhelmed by hardship, perhaps the best way to respond is to go to our Prince of Peace, curl up beside Him, and rest "undisturbed in the midst of the disturbance."

There will always be storms in life, but God is our Immanuel, and He wants us to have a strong, empowering faith that compels us to live confidently, trusting in His love, His ways, and His faithfulness. God is always enough, but we have the choice of believing whether He is enough or He is not.

PERSONAL THOUGHTS AND REFLECTIONS

Quiet your heart and pray Hebrews 13:6: "We can say with confidence, 'The LORD is my helper, so I will have no fear.'" Ask the Lord to guide you as you prayerfully meditate on this chapter.

9. Review the Scriptures and your answers and record what truths or special thoughts stood out to you.

10. What have you learned about faith in this chapter?

11. What do you think Jesus meant when He said, "Take heart!" (John 16:33, MSG)?

12. How do you respond when overwhelmed by circumstances?

13. How do you see God strengthening and protecting your spirit through trials?

14. When you are in the midst of a storm, what helps to calm your fears and silence your doubts?

15. Can you say with the psalmist, "Even if I am attacked, I will remain confident" (Psalm 27:3)? Why or why not?

16. What personal application can you make as a result of studying this chapter?

17. Close your time of reflection by praying over Psalm 86:1-13.

The problem of reconciling human suffering with the existence of a God who loves, is only insoluble so long as we attach a trivial meaning to the word "love," and look on things as if man were the centre of them. Man is not the centre. God does not exist for the sake of man. Man does not exist for his own sake. "Thou hast created all things, and for thy pleasure they are created" [Revelation 4:11]. We were made not primarily that we may love God (though we were made for that too) but that God may love us, that we may become objects in which the Divine love may rest "well pleased." To ask that God's love should be content with us as we are is to ask that God should cease to be God: because He is what He is, His love must, in the nature of things, be impeded and repelled by certain stains in our present character, and because He always loves us He must labour to make us lovable.[15]

C. S. LEWIS

 SCRIPTURE MEMORY

MATTHEW 8:26—*Jesus responded, "Why are you afraid? You have so little faith!"*

God is Enough

let the Lord be your Shepherd
pray & wait Isiah 30:21
30:21

Janet
4:13-15

Ephesians 2:10
Psalm 25:10, 33:3, 43:8
Jeremiah 29:11
Romans 8:32

Psalm
23

AUTHee - GATHer

Genesis 13:5-7, 8-9, 10-11
13:14-17

When we let God choose
for us, he Gives
his choice for me

When in doubt, Don't !!

CHAPTER 8

GOD CHOOSES FOR YOU

Cynthia Heald ~~Heald~~ *—author*

Come now, you who say, "Today or tomorrow we will go into such and such a town and spend a year there and trade and make a profit"—yet you do not know what tomorrow will bring. What is your life? For you are a mist that appears for a little time and then vanishes. Instead you ought to say, "If the Lord wills, we will live and do this or that."

JAMES 4:13-15, ESV

As soon as you begin to live the life of faith in God, fascinating and luxurious prospects will open up before you, and these things are yours by right; but if you are living the life of faith you will exercise your right to waive your rights, and let God choose for you.

OSWALD CHAMBERS, *My Utmost for His Highest*

A. W. TOZER WROTE THESE challenging words: "God has charged Himself with full responsibility for our eternal happiness and stands ready to take over the management of our lives the moment we turn in faith to Him."[1] We have studied God as the self-existent One, our Shepherd, Redeemer, Protector, and Provider. We know of His great love and grace. We understand that His purpose in our lives is Christlikeness. God is the almighty God, and only He, who created us, can know what is best for us.

God, "who did not spare his own Son but gave him up for us all, . . . will he not also . . . give us all things" (Romans 8:32, ESV)? And since He gave the highest and best in giving His Son, what makes us think that He will not continue to give us the best? How it must grieve our Lord to stand by and watch us manage our own lives and in the process make wrong choices—choices that may have lifelong repercussions. Yet, no matter how long we have chosen our own way, no matter what circumstances we might be in, God stands ready to take over for us. It is in believing that God is enough that we can turn in faith to Him and give Him permission to choose His path for us—the path that is always the most suitable, the most honorable, the most advantageous, the most blessed, the *best*.

As Jim Elliot said, "God always gives His best to those who leave the choice with Him."[2]

❦ GOD'S WAYS ARE BEST

1. Concerning his next visit to the Corinthian church, Paul made this statement, "This time I don't want to make just a short visit and then go right on. I want to come and stay awhile, if the Lord will let me" (1 Corinthians 16:7). Just as Paul was willing to let the Lord choose for him, James reiterated this concept in James 4:13-17. Study these verses and comment on the reasons we should depend on God rather than ourselves to guide us.

We do not know what tomorrow brings.— I forget to ask God for help—Instead I should always say— Lord willing

Certainty is the mark of the common-sense life: gracious uncertainty is the mark of the spiritual life. To be certain of God means that we are uncertain in all our ways, we do not know what a day may bring forth. . . . But when we are rightly related to God, life is full of spontaneous, joyful uncertainty and expectancy.[3] OSWALD CHAMBERS

2. Scripture faithfully recounts the lives of those whose stories it tells. As we study the choices these men and women made, perhaps we can learn from them about the consequences of selfish choices and the blessings of trusting God to go before us. Read the Scriptures and fill in the appropriate column.

Person	Choice	Consequence
Lot Genesis 13:1-13		
Ruth Ruth 2:1-12; 4:13-17		
David 2 Samuel 12:1-12		
Gehazi (servant to Elisha when Naaman was healed) 2 Kings 5:15-16, 20-27		
The Rich Fool Luke 12:13-21		

3. Oswald Chambers noted, "A Christian is someone who trusts in the knowledge and the wisdom of God, not in his own abilities." [4] As you reflect on the above passages, write a summary of the implications of managing your own life.

❧ GOD'S BEST IS WRAPPED IN LOVE

4. One of the most notable psalms is David's Psalm 139. It beautifully depicts God's omniscience and divine knowledge. Read Psalm 139:16 and comment on the various manifestations of God's intimate knowledge of us.

--- ☙ ---

If we cannot escape His observant eye, so too we cannot be hid from His vigilant love. He loved His people before their members were framed, and never has His love relaxed. [5]

HENRY LAW

5. Oswald Chambers frequently taught how God wants to help Himself to our lives. As you read these verses, what encouragement do you receive to let God help Himself to your life?

PSALM 25:8-10 ·· ⌒

PSALM 32:8 ·· ⌒

2 CORINTHIANS 5:15 ······································· ⌒

———————— ⌒ ————————

God expects us to use our brains and make plans, but He also expects us to submit those plans to Him and let Him make the final decision. . . . So when we have a decision to make, we gather all the facts and seek wise counsel, we make our plans, we commit ourselves and our plans to the Lord, we listen to His Word, and we wait before Him for His leading. Sometimes God leads us through a Bible promise or warning; sometimes while we're at worship with God's people, He speaks through a song or Scripture reading; or He may direct us through providential circumstances.[6]

WARREN W. WIERSBE

6. "We may dwell 'with the king for his work' anywhere and everywhere. We may be called to serve Him in the most unlikely places and under the most adverse conditions."[7] God often places us in circumstances that we might not choose for ourselves. What can you learn from these passages about being faithful to God in your present circumstances?

LUKE 2:36-38

ACTS 9:36-41

ACTS 20:22-24

———————— ❧ ————————

Notice God's unutterable waste of saints, according to the judgment of the world. God plants His saints in the most useless places. We say—God intends me to be here because I am so useful. Jesus never estimated His life along the line of the greatest use. God puts His saints where they will glorify Him, and we are no judges at all of where that is.[8]

OSWALD CHAMBERS

SCRIPTURAL RESPONSES TO GOD'S SUFFICIENCY

When God Didn't Seem to Be Enough

ISRAEL

> *All the elders of Israel met at Ramah to discuss the matter with Samuel. "Look," they told him, "you are now old, and your sons are not like you. Give us a king to judge us like all the other nations have." Samuel was displeased with their request and went to the LORD for guidance. "Do everything they say to you," the LORD replied, "for they are rejecting me, not you. They don't want me to be their king any longer. Ever since I brought them from Egypt they have continually abandoned me and followed other gods. And now they are giving you the same treatment. Do as they ask, but solemnly warn them about the way a king will reign over them."* I SAMUEL 8:4-9

When God Was Enough

ESTHER

King Xerxes ruled Persia from 486–465 BC. He chose his queen, Esther, mainly for her beauty, and was unaware that she was of Jewish lineage. Haman, the king's evil prime minister, convinced Xerxes to sign a decree to exterminate all the Jews in the country because he was jealous of Esther's uncle, Mordecai. When Mordecai received news of the edict, he urged Esther to intercede for her people before the king. Esther, who had not been in the king's presence for a month, was hesitant to approach him because of the Persian law that forbade anyone from entering the king's presence uninvited. If anyone appeared unexpectedly and the king did not extend his golden scepter, that person could be put to death. Nonetheless Mordecai implored Esther to intervene, and he reminded her that "perhaps you were made queen for just such a time as this" (Esther 4:14).

> *Esther sent this reply to Mordecai: "Go and gather together all the Jews of Susa and fast for me. Do not eat or drink for three days, night or day. My maids and I will do the same. And then, though it is against the law, I will go in to see the king. If I must die, I must die." So Mordecai went away and did everything as Esther had ordered him. On the third day of the fast, Esther put on her royal robes and entered the inner court of the palace, just across from the king's hall. The king was sitting on his royal throne, facing the entrance. When he saw Queen Esther standing there in the inner court, he welcomed her and held out the gold scepter to her. So Esther approached and touched the end of the scepter.*
>
> ESTHER 4:15–5:2

(This story has a happy ending! Esther speaks to the king, the Jews are permitted to defend themselves, and they ultimately triumph.)

7. Chambers reminds us that "if you are living the life of faith you exercise your right to waive your rights, and let God choose for you."[9] Contrast the process Esther chose in relinquishing her rights with the way Israel chose to have a king. What can you learn from these passages?

THOUGHTS AND REFLECTIONS FROM AN OLDER WOMAN

When I was twenty-six years old, I exercised my right to waive my rights and surrendered my life to the Lord. When I turned forty, I was surprised at how quickly the years had passed, and I realized that in all probability my life was half over. I was familiar with James 4:14, which teaches that life is like mist: here for only a little while. I told the Lord, "I don't know how many years I have left, but I want You to know that for the rest of my life, I always want to be in the center of Your will."

It was a renewal of my desire to let God choose for me. As I began my Bible reading that year, I became intrigued with Ruth 3:11, where Boaz said to Ruth, "Now, my daughter, do not fear. I will do for you whatever you ask, for all my people in the city know that you are a woman of excellence" (NASB). When I read that verse, I told the Lord, "I'm not sure what a woman of excellence is, but I want to find out. And I want to spend the rest of my life becoming a woman of excellence for Your glory."

It took a few years (I had four teenagers at the time), but I wrote a course entitled *Becoming a Woman of Excellence* for the women at our church. I taught it for a couple of years, and then a friend heard about it and, without my knowledge, arranged an appointment for me with an editor from NavPress.

The rest is history. The study was published, and ever since I have been writing and speaking at seminars. I tell this story because I never really prayed about or planned to write or speak. I continue to be taken aback when I am introduced as the speaker. Also, I am not a writer. Writing is extremely hard for me. My view of writing is "chaining myself to the computer."

I know that it can sound glamorous to write, speak, and travel. But for me, writing is demanding and difficult work that requires discipline and something to say! One day as I sat down to write, I began to pray for wisdom and guidance. In my silence I was convicted as I heard these thoughts from the Lord: *Oh, Cynthia, I view your study and writing as our special times of communion.* Travel can be very stressful and, at times, frustrating. Yet, this is His handpicked path for me to grow in intimacy with Him and to stay wholly dependent upon Him. I am on this path because, thankfully, I waived my rights, placed my hand in His, and gave Him permission to choose for me.

As I look back over this path that God chose for me, I realize that He has used my writing and studying primarily to teach, correct, and train me. Truly, each study has transformed my life in a multitude of ways. I have no favorite study—each one has uniquely drawn me closer to the Lord and increased my love for Him.

Perhaps you may just be learning about the sufficiency of God and the desire of the Lord to choose the best path for you. It is never too late to let God work. He is our Shepherd who restores our souls (Psalm 23:3). He is our Savior who gives "a crown of beauty for ashes, a joyous blessing instead of mourning, festive praise instead of despair" (Isaiah 61:3). Jeremiah reminds us: "The faithful love of the LORD never ends! His mercies never cease. Great is his faithfulness; his mercies begin afresh each morning" (Lamentations 3:22-23). It is because of God's mercies, love, and faithfulness that He wants to choose what is best for you.

Mike Mason summarized this thought well: "What we fail to understand is that the moment we give our will to God, He gives it right back to us again. Are we frightened that if we surrender our will, we shall end up without a will at all? But then we would be nonpersons and useless to God. No, the Christian secret is that the only way we can have a will at all, properly speaking, is by giving it to God, so that He can cleanse it, renew it, and restore it to us fully intact."[10]

Queen Esther and Jim Elliot, martyred missionary in Ecuador, were both willing to let God choose for them, even if it meant they might die. Both kept an eternal perspective on life, and as His servants, they trusted in His will for them.

The God who knows everything about you, who is ever-present, who made all the delicate, inner parts of your body, and who has recorded each of your days in His book, is the God who is enough to choose your path—for He always gives His best to those who leave the choice to Him.

PERSONAL THOUGHTS AND REFLECTIONS

Pray the following verse: "How precious are your thoughts about me, O God. They cannot be numbered!" (Psalm 139:17). Take a few moments to quiet your heart and to thank the Lord for His intimate knowledge and love for you.

8. Carefully review this chapter and note the Scriptures or quotations that stood out to you.

9. How does understanding the brevity of life help you in letting God choose for you?

10. What does exercising "your right to waive your rights" mean to you?

11. Which biblical character and the choices he or she made had an impact on you? Why?

12. Are you encouraged by knowing that you can serve and glorify God in commonplace circumstances? Why or why not?

13. Ask God to pinpoint the ways you tend to manage your life. Be still in His presence in order to discern what you need to do to allow Him to choose for you.

14. As you meditate on James 4:13-17, take time to substitute *I* for *you* and *my* for *your* in order to make these verses more personal.

15. Close by praying the words of Psalm 139:23-24.

Beloved, whenever you are in doubt as to which way to turn, submit your judgment absolutely to the Spirit of God, asking Him to shut every door but the right one. Say to Him, "Blessed Spirit, I give to You the entire responsibility of closing every road and stopping every step that is not of God. Let me hear Your voice behind me whenever I 'turn aside to the right or to the left.' [Deut. 5:32]."[11]　F. B. MEYER

SCRIPTURE MEMORY

JAMES 4:13-15—*Come now, you who say, "Today or tomorrow we will go into such and such a town and spend a year there and trade and make a profit"—yet you do not know what tomorrow will bring. What is your life? For you are a mist that appears for a little time and then vanishes. Instead you ought to say, "If the Lord wills, we will live and do this or that." (ESV)*

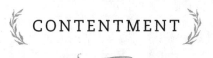 CONTENTMENT

Not that I was ever in need, for I have learned how to be content with whatever I have.

PHILIPPIANS 4:11

Christian contentment is that sweet, inward, quiet, gracious frame of spirit, which freely submits to and delights in God's wise and fatherly disposal in every condition.

JEREMIAH BURROUGHS, *The Rare Jewel of Christian Contentment*

JEREMIAH BURROUGHS, A WELL-KNOWN ENGLISH puritan preacher, wrote the above definition of contentment in 1648. In his excellent book, *The Rare Jewel of Christian Contentment*, Burroughs declared a profound truth: "When a Christian is content in the right way, the quiet comes more from the temper and disposition of the heart than from any external argument or from the possession of anything in the world."[1] Warren Wiersbe made this observation: "The word *contentment* means 'an inner sufficiency that keeps us at peace in spite of outward circumstances.'"[2]

It was Paul's "gracious frame of spirit" that enabled him to write, "I've learned by now to be quite content whatever my circumstances.

I'm just as happy with little as with much, with much as with little"
(Philippians 4:12, MSG). Understanding that people, things, or circumstances do not determine our contentment is a priceless gift for
our souls. Knowing that the determining factor of contentment is
the disposition of our hearts frees us from striving, comparing, and
being discontent. But this sweet, gracious perspective is something
to be learned.

Certainly, one essential way to learn this lesson is by believing
and allowing God to be enough for us. For if He is our Shepherd
who provides all we need, and if He gives all things freely and for
our good, then we cannot help but be content.

🌿 LEARNING CONTENTMENT

1. Part of learning about any subject is to take time to discover
   the underlying principles supporting your chosen topic. As
   you look up these verses, write down the fundamental truths
   that are necessary in acquiring contentment.

   PHILIPPIANS 4:11-13 ·· ᘒ

   COLOSSIANS 3:5 ··· ᘒ

1 TIMOTHY 6:6-12 ....

HEBREWS 13:5 ....

---

*The Greek word behind covetousness (*pleonexia*) is defined as "the state of desiring to have more than one's due," which is to say that a covetous person is not content with what they've been allotted by God—including God himself—and so they are constantly looking elsewhere for their satisfaction.*[3]

TIM CHALLIES

2. Asaph penned one of my favorite psalms—Psalm 73. Read this psalm and summarize his journey of learning to be content with God alone.

Paul said he had learned to be content. He recognized it was his responsibility to be content, and that he needed to grow in that area of life. He didn't just turn it all over to the Lord and trust Him to do the work of being content. He worked at it. But he knew that he could be content only through the Lord, who gave him strength.[4]   JERRY BRIDGES

3. Paul's secret of contentment was the confidence he had in Christ's sufficiency and strength for every circumstance. Record your thoughts about how Christ's power and presence in your life nurture contentment.

 LIVING A CONTENTED LIFE

4. Although people and circumstances do not dictate our contentment, they can offer challenging lessons in the process of learning to be content. Responding in a godly way to these tests can be a measure of our gracious frame of spirit. What can you learn from these passages about the unfavorable behavior of a discontented person?

——————— ❧ ———————

Really, it's never about those outer things, even those profoundly good outer things; contentment doesn't come through a sentimental inventory of the blessings in this life. The abundant good I've known has never (yet) been stripped away leaving me with no visible reason for joy. And still, discontentment has the power to grab hold and infect, dragging me to a place of joylessness and sin, taking what is lovely and making it seem worthless. . . . The path

out of discontentment is not through beholding all that may be
good or beautiful in my situation. The path to contentment, after
repentance, is remembering who I am in Christ.[5]

ELISHA GALOTTI

5. Paul said he learned to be content with little or much. Our contentment level is not dictated by the amount of our worldly goods. How do these Scriptures help you have the proper view and use of your possessions?

PROVERBS 15:16 ....

PROVERBS 30:7-9 ....

1 TIMOTHY 6:17-19 ....

6. Evelyn Underhill wrote, "This is the secret of joy. We shall no longer strive for our own way; but commit ourselves, easily and simply, to God's way, acquiesce in his will and in so doing find our peace."[6] How do these Scriptures encourage you to commit yourself to God's way?

PSALM 131 ....

LUKE 9:23-25 ....

If a man is selfish and self-love prevails in his heart, he will be glad of those things that suit with his own ends, but a godly man who has denied himself will suit with and be glad of all things that shall suit with God's ends. A gracious heart says, God's ends are my ends and I have denied my own ends; so he comes to find contentment in all God's ends and ways, and his comforts are multiplied, whereas the comforts of other men are single.[7] JEREMIAH BURROUGHS

7. J. Hudson Taylor, pioneer missionary to China, declared, "I know He tries me only to increase my faith, and that is all in love. Well, if He is glorified, I am content."[8] For Taylor, God's glory is an aspect of contentment. Reflect on John 9:1-3 and John 11:1-7. Express your ideas about how desiring to bring glory to God can contribute to being content with your circumstances.

The Scotch catechism says that man's chief end is "to glorify God and enjoy Him forever." But we shall then know that these are the same thing. Fully to enjoy is to glorify. In commanding us to glorify Him, God is inviting us to enjoy Him.[9]   C. S. LEWIS

SCRIPTURAL RESPONSES TO GOD'S SUFFICIENCY

When God Didn't Seem to Be Enough

ANANIAS

There was a certain man named Ananias who, with his wife, Sapphira, sold some property. He brought part of the money to the apostles, claiming it was the full amount. With his wife's consent, he kept the rest. Then Peter said, "Ananias, why have you let Satan fill your heart? You lied to the Holy Spirit, and you kept some of the money for yourself. The property was yours to sell or not sell, as you wished. And after selling it, the money was also yours to give away. How could you do a thing like this? You weren't lying to us but to God!" As soon as Ananias heard these words, he fell to the floor and died.   ACTS 5:1-5

When God Was Enough

THE WIDOW OF ZAREPHATH

The Lord directed Elijah to go and live in the village of Zarephath, where a widow would feed him. When Elijah asked for food, the widow replied that she had only a handful of flour and a little oil left. She was preparing to cook a last meal for her son and herself, and then they would die.

Elijah said to her, "Don't be afraid! Go ahead and do just what you've said, but make a little bread for me first. Then use what's left to prepare a meal for yourself and your son. For this is what the LORD, the God of Israel, says: There will always be flour and olive oil left in your containers until the time when the LORD sends rain and the crops grow again!" So she did as Elijah said, and she and Elijah and her family continued to eat for many days. There was always enough flour and olive oil left in the containers, just as the LORD had promised through Elijah.

I KINGS 17:13-16

8. The Greek sage and Stoic philosopher Epictetus stated, "Fortify yourself with contentment, for this is an impregnable fortress."[10] After reflecting on the above passages, express your thoughts concerning Epictetus' view that contentment is a protective safeguard in our lives.

THOUGHTS AND REFLECTIONS FROM AN OLDER WOMAN

The accepted definition of contentment is being satisfied with one's situation. A wise person amplified the meaning of contentment with this observation: *Contentment is being satisfied—satisfied not because something is in sufficient supply, but satisfied with whatever is available.* This definition seems to be more realistic, for we seldom get to stay in circumstances that are ideal. Hebrews 13:5 verifies this thought: "Be satisfied with what you have." To be content with where we are, who we are, and what we have does not come naturally. This satisfaction is something to be learned, and the lessons often come through trying situations.

Recently I experienced a rather exhausting night because of a delayed flight. My husband and I arrived at the Denver airport at 11:30 p.m. All the gates were closed and all the motels were full. So we laid our jackets on the airport floor and tried to rest. It was a long, sleepless night. (Who knew that huge, noisy vacuum cleaners were used to sweep the carpets?) As I lay awake, I recalled the definition of contentment—being content with what is available. What was available was a carpeted floor in an airport. Since circumstances are not the measure of contentment, I chose to calm and quiet myself like a weaned child. In accepting this unexpected and unwanted event, I prayed, "Lord, these are my circumstances—I can't change them, and they are all that are available; therefore, I choose to be content."

On some level, experiencing true contentment will usually involve denying ourselves. Jeremiah Burroughs taught,

> The lesson of self-denial. It is a hard lesson. You know that when a child is first taught, he complains: This is hard; it is just like that. I remember Bradford the martyr said, "Whoever has not learned the lesson of the cross, has not learned his ABC in Christianity." This is where Christ begins with his scholars, and those in the lowest form must begin with this; if you mean to be Christians at all, you must buckle to this or you can never be Christians. Just as no-one can be a scholar

unless he learns his ABC, so you must learn the lesson of self-denial or you can never become a scholar in Christ's school, and be learned in this mystery of contentment.[11]

Revelation 1:5 encourages us: "All glory to him who loves us and has freed us from our sins by shedding his blood for us." Focusing on God's grace, love, and sacrifice is instrumental in learning contentment and helps us to look at life with an eternal perspective. Again, Jeremiah Burroughs gave these insights:

> Before, the soul sought after this and that, but now it says, I see that it is not necessary for me to be rich, but it is necessary for me to make my peace with God; it is not necessary that I should live a pleasurable life in this world, but it is absolutely necessary that I should have pardon of my sin; it is not necessary that I should have honour and preferment, but it is necessary that I should have God as my portion, and have my part in Jesus Christ, it is necessary that my soul should be saved in the day of Jesus Christ.[12]

Essentially the secret of contentment is the Cross. The spiritual riches that are ours in Christ strengthen and free us to be content in the world—with little or much. "He who did not spare his own Son but gave him up for us all, how will he not also with him graciously give us all things?" (Romans 8:32, ESV).

*God is most glorified in you when you are most satisfied
in Him.*[13]
SAMUEL STORMS

 PERSONAL THOUGHTS AND REFLECTIONS

As you enter into a time of contemplation, pray Psalm 73:25-26:
"Whom have I in heaven but you? I desire you more than anything
on earth. My health may fail, and my spirit may grow weak, but
God remains the strength of my heart; he is mine forever."

9. As you look over this chapter, highlight any special Scriptures
   or quotations that ministered to you.

10. How do you define contentment in your life?

11. What was an outstanding truth about contentment that im-
    pressed you? Why?

12. What aspects of your life do you feel need to be addressed in order to be content?

13. Specify the principles that can help you learn contentment.

14. Pinpoint any red flags or manifestations in your behavior that can serve to warn you that you are traveling on the path to discontentment.

15. Close in prayer by expressing your desire to excel as a scholar in Christ's school, especially in the course on contentment. Assure the Lord that you want to learn contentment and that you desire to delight in His wise and fatherly disposals in every condition. Ask that you can have the great wealth that results from true godliness and a contented heart. Pray that you will be a good steward of what you have. Tell the Lord that you want the disposition of your heart to be centered in Him and that you desire to depend upon His strength to live through every situation in order to bring Him glory. Thank Him for His sacrifice and for the spiritual riches that are yours. Praise

Him that one of the "all things" that He so graciously gives is contentment.

You don't realize Jesus is all you need until Jesus is all you have.[14]

TIMOTHY KELLER

 SCRIPTURE MEMORY

PHILIPPIANS 4:11—*Not that I was ever in need, for I have learned how to be content with whatever I have.*

 HUMILITY

Take my yoke upon you. Let me teach you, because I am humble and gentle at heart, and you will find rest for your souls. For my yoke is easy to bear, and the burden I give you is light.

MATTHEW 11:29-30

Meekness and lowliness of heart are the chief marks by which they who follow the Lamb of God are to be known.

ANDREW MURRAY, *Humility*

WE BEGAN OUR STUDY WITH the premise that the last and greatest lesson to be learned is the fact that God and God alone is enough for all our needs. When I fully comprehend God's graciousness and personal love and care for me, I cannot help but bow in humility before Him. He is our almighty God, and the natural by-product of my learning this lesson of His sufficiency is humble dependence upon Him. Accepting the yoke of Christ is a crucial step in letting God be enough. Taking His yoke signifies our yielding control of our lives and trusting Him to lead and guide us; it indicates our total reliance upon Him to meet all our needs. Being yoked to the Lord allows us to become like Him— gentle and humble.

In Matthew 11:29-30 we have a personal invitation from the Lord to join Him in His yoke. "To 'take a yoke' in that day meant to become a disciple. When we submit to Christ, we are yoked to Him."[1] The Lord contrasted His light and easy yoke with the legalistic and oppressive law or "yoke" of the Pharisees. The Pharisees, as teachers, were harsh and inflexible, and they laid heavy burdens of religious responsibilities on their disciples; Jesus, though, was meek and lowly of heart and offered rest and a light burden.

We are familiar with the definition of *humility* that describes someone as having a "modest opinion of one's own importance or rank; meekness."[2] Jesus described Himself as gentle and humble; the King James Version of Matthew 11:29 uses "meek and lowly in heart." *Meek* in the Greek means mild and gentle. We tend to think of one who is meek as insecure and passive. But Warren Wiersbe explained meekness in this way: "Meekness is not weakness, for both Moses and Jesus were meek men (Numbers 12:3; Matthew 11:29). This word translated 'meek' was used by the Greeks to describe a horse that had been broken. It refers to power under control."[3]

Humility is a joyful dependence upon God for all that is needed; it is a glad surrender to the will of God; it is unpretentious, gentle, and more thoughtful of others than of self. In this chapter we will be reminded of the blessings of humility.

❧ THE HUMILITY OF GOD

1. A good teacher exemplifies what he teachers. Jesus described Himself as being humble and gentle. As you read these Scriptures, record the ways Jesus demonstrated humility.

ZECHARIAH 9:9 ···

MATTHEW 20:28 ···

JOHN 13:3-17 ···

PHILIPPIANS 2:5-8 ···

--------------------- ❧ ---------------------

If you are looking for an example of humility, look at the cross.[4]   THOMAS AQUINAS

2. Jesus chose lowly fisherman to be His key disciples. This in itself testifies to God's humility. How do the following verses confirm God's love for the humble?

PSALM 25:9 ··

ISAIAH 57:15 ··

ISAIAH 66:2 ··

MATTHEW 5:5 ··

———————— ⌘ ————————

Isn't it interesting that God did not choose to live with the wise people, the rich people or the super strong people. As great as God is you would have thought He would have enjoyed their company more. On earth we tend to gravitate to people who think like we do and have similar ideas. But then it occurred to me that maybe that is the whole reason. Who could be more humble than God? . . . What could be more humbling than to take upon yourself the likeness of a mere human being, walk among us with all our limitations and then die for us? That is why He dwells with ones who know what *they are (corrupt to the core) and* who *they are (a complex human created by Him). First Corinthians 4:7 states it plainly: "What makes you better than anyone else? What do you have that God hasn't given you? And if all you have is from God, why boast as if you have accomplished something on your own?"*[5]   BARBARA MADISON

3. Andrew Murray summed up humility in this way: "Humility is nothing but the disappearance of self in the vision that God is all."[6] Reflect on the above questions and write a brief paragraph expressing your thoughts about why humility is so highly regarded in God's sight.

⚜ THE TEACHING OF HUMILITY

4. The ways the Lord teaches us to be humble are creative and filled with surprising assignments. As you study these

Scriptures, write down some of the ways God uses to teach humility.

DEUTERONOMY 8:1-3 ....

MATTHEW 18:1-4 ....

HEBREWS 5:8 ....

There is no harder lesson to learn than the lesson of humility. It is not taught in the schools of men, only in the school of Christ. It is the rarest of all the gifts. Very rarely do we find a man or woman who is following closely the footsteps of the Master in meekness and in humility. I believe that it is the hardest lesson which Jesus Christ had to teach His disciples while He was here upon earth. It almost looked at first as though He had failed to teach it to the twelve men who had been with Him almost constantly for three years.[7]

DWIGHT L. MOODY

THE HUMILITY OF A DISCIPLE

5. Ephesians 4:2 teaches, "Always be humble and gentle." What are some of the essential characteristics of humility found in these passages?

MATTHEW 5:3 ···

PHILIPPIANS 2:3-4 ··

COLOSSIANS 3:12-14 ···

1 PETER 3:8-9 ··

There is no limit to what God can do through you, provided you do not seek your own glory.[8]   ANONYMOUS

6. John Chrysostom wrote, "Humility is the root, mother, nurse, foundation, and bond of all virtue."[9] Proverbs 11:2 notes, "Pride leads to disgrace, but with humility comes wisdom." What wisdom can you learn from these verses concerning the "bond of all virtue"?

MATTHEW 23:11-12 .... ❧

MARK 10:35-45 .... ❧

1 PETER 5:5-6 .... ❧

7. The path of humility is paved by godly men and women who were willing to humble themselves under the mighty hand of God. How is their humility revealed in these Scriptures?

GENESIS 41:14-16 • *Joseph* .... ❧

EXODUS 3:11; NUMBERS 12:3 • *Moses* .... ⚬

1 CHRONICLES 29:13-14 • *David* .... ⚬

EPHESIANS 3:8 • *Paul* .... ⚬

⸻⸻ ⚬⚬ ⸻⸻

The proper way to become humble is not to run myself down trying to belittle myself. Rather, I need to stand straight and tall, recognizing my strengths and abilities, but standing next to the Lord Jesus so that I can see myself in true perspective. It was William Temple who wrote, "Humility does not mean thinking less of yourself than of other people, nor does it mean having a low opinion of your own gifts. It means freedom from thinking about yourself one way or the other at all." That is true, but it stops short of telling how *not to think of ourselves. The answer is that we are to fill our minds with the Lord Jesus. It is worship that drives out arrogance and pours in love.*[10]
GARY INRIG

SCRIPTURAL RESPONSES TO GOD'S SUFFICIENCY

When God Didn't Seem to Be Enough

KING UZZIAH

Uzziah was king of Israel. He ruled for fifty-two years and did what was pleasing to the Lord during the days of Zechariah, who taught him to fear God. Second Chronicles 26:5 notes, "As long as the king sought guidance from the LORD, God gave him success."

> *When he had become powerful, he also became proud, which led to his downfall. He sinned against the LORD his God by entering the sanctuary of the LORD's Temple and personally burning incense on the incense altar. Azariah the high priest went in after him with eighty other priests of the LORD, all brave men. They confronted King Uzziah and said, "It is not for you, Uzziah, to burn incense to the LORD. That is the work of the priests alone, the descendants of Aaron who are set apart for this work. Get out of the sanctuary, for you have sinned. The LORD God will not honor you for this!" Uzziah, who was holding an incense burner, became furious. But as he was standing there raging at the priests before the incense altar in the LORD's Temple, leprosy suddenly broke out on his forehead. . . . So King Uzziah had leprosy until the day he died.*
>
> 2 CHRONICLES 26:16-19, 21

When God Was Enough

JOHN THE BAPTIST

The Jewish leaders asked John, "Who are you?"

> *John replied in the words of the prophet Isaiah: "I am a voice shouting in the wilderness, 'Clear the way for the LORD's*

coming!'" Then the Pharisees who had been sent asked him, "If
you aren't the Messiah or Elijah or the Prophet, what right do
you have to baptize?" John told them, "I baptize with water, but
right here in the crowd is someone you do not recognize. Though
his ministry follows mine, I'm not even worthy to be his slave and
untie the straps of his sandal." JOHN 1:23-27

A debate broke out between John's disciples and a certain Jew over
ceremonial cleansing. So John's disciples came to him and said,
"Rabbi, the man you met on the other side of the Jordan River, the
one you identified as the Messiah, is also baptizing people. And
everybody is going to him instead of coming to us." John replied,
"No one can receive anything unless God gives it from heaven. You
yourselves know how plainly I told you, 'I am not the Messiah.
I am only here to prepare the way for him.' It is the bridegroom
who marries the bride, and the bridegroom's friend is simply glad
to stand with him and hear his vows. Therefore, I am filled with
joy at his success. He must become greater and greater, and I must
become less and less." JOHN 3:25-30

8. G. K. Chesterton remarked, "It is always the secure who are humble."[11] How do you see this thought exemplified in the lives of King Uzziah and John the Baptist?

THOUGHTS AND REFLECTIONS
FROM AN OLDER WOMAN

I was challenged by D. L. Moody's observation that humility and meekness are uncommon among Christ's disciples. The following anonymous quotation made me smile: "Many would be scantily clad if clothed in humility."[12] Yet if we are Christ's disciples and yoked to Him, the qualities of humility and gentleness should be evident to everyone we meet. One of my favorite verses is Philippians 4:5: "Let your gentleness be known to all men" (NKJV).

Jesus taught, "The student who is fully trained will become like the teacher" (Luke 6:40). Louis Evely beautifully described the life of a disciple in this way:

> Christianity is neither contemplation nor action. It is
> participation. Contemplation is looking at God as if He
> were an object. But if you participate in God in the sense
> that you let yourself be penetrated by Him you will go
> to the cross like Him, you will go to work like Him, you
> will clean shoes, do the washing up and the cooking, all
> like Him. You cannot do otherwise because you will have
> become part of Him. You will do what He loves to do.[13]

A few thoughts about false humility: William Law said, "You can have no greater sign of confirmed pride than when you think you are humble enough."[14] And Saint Cyran, a French theologian, remarked, "There is no greater pride than in seeking to humiliate ourselves beyond measure; and sometimes there is no truer humility than to attempt great works for God."[15] Finally, Meryl Streep: "You can't get spoiled if you do your own ironing."[16]

Chesterton's view that only a secure person can be humble is enlightening. John the Baptist embodied this idea, for he was secure and confident in his calling and purpose in life. Jesus praised and exalted John by telling the crowds, "I tell you the truth, of all who have ever lived, none is greater than John the Baptist" (Matthew 11:11). Someone observed, "Humility is the acceptance of the place appointed by God, whether it be in the front or in the rear."[17]

It was in 1988 that I attended a Christian Booksellers Association convention. That year the study *Becoming a Woman of Excellence* was among the top ten bestselling books. I was told that an article was being written about the authors of these books, and I was to be interviewed at a certain time. When I sat down with the reporter, she asked, "Now, what is the name of your book?" The first thing I said was, "Oh, actually it's really not a book, it is a Bible study." She looked at me and said, "Well, if it is not a book, I do not need to interview you." She rose from her seat and promptly left.

This event left an indelible imprint on my soul. It was God's lesson for me to keep a proper perspective on my writing and any praise I might receive. Humility is the acceptance of the place appointed to us by God, so I am thankful that from the beginning of my literary career, I was given this experience to keep me from thinking more highly of myself than I should. Paul warned the Corinthian church: "Don't cherish exaggerated ideas of yourself or your importance, but try to have a sane estimate of your capabilities by the light of the faith that God has given to you all" (Romans 12:3, PH).

I can look back over my life and see the Lord's hand and purpose in the countless "meekness-producing" lessons I have been given and continue to have. Apart from His yoke, though, I fear I would be prone to cherish exaggerated ideas of myself.

Being yoked to Christ is a beautiful picture of humble dependence, intimacy, and self-denial. Connected to Christ, we lose all sense of self and desire only to know Him and to do His will. Self is no longer in control, self is no longer seeking prestige, approval, comfort, or possessions. It is no longer defensive. It is teachable, gentle, and thoughtful of others. At last we are secure. Our strength is under Christ's control and we begin a thrilling life of continually being transformed into His likeness. Christ's yoke offers freedom—freedom to rest in who we are, whose we are, and where we are—whether the front or the rear—for no matter our lot, God is enough.

I was deeply moved when I heard about a graduating class that chose the janitor of their Christian high school to be the speaker for their baccalaureate service. I thought that this dear humble man must have quietly and profoundly befriended and served those students. Apparently, it was evident that he was yoked to Christ, for he exemplified the chief marks by which those who follow the Lamb of God are to be known: meekness and lowliness of heart.

❧ PERSONAL THOUGHTS AND REFLECTIONS

Begin by praying Psalm 62:1-2: "I wait quietly before God, for my victory comes from him. He alone is my rock and my salvation, my fortress where I will never be shaken."

9.   Look over this chapter and note any special Scriptures or thoughts that caught your attention.

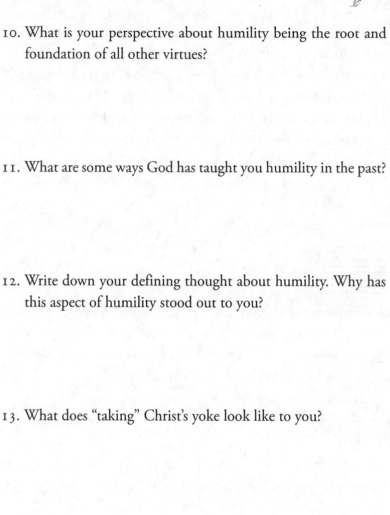

10. What is your perspective about humility being the root and foundation of all other virtues?

11. What are some ways God has taught you humility in the past?

12. Write down your defining thought about humility. Why has this aspect of humility stood out to you?

13. What does "taking" Christ's yoke look like to you?

14. What practical steps can you take to ensure that you continue to grow in humility?

15. Close by writing out a prayer expressing your desire to have humility and gentleness be the chief marks of your character. Tell Him of your longing to be totally dependent upon Him and that you will gladly accept His yoke. Praise Him for His gentleness and humility and for His love for those who are humble and contrite. Pray that you will be steadfast and that you will soon become fully trained so as to be like your Teacher.

I shall recommend humility to you as highly proper to be made the constant subject of your devotions, earnestly desiring you to think no day safe, or likely to end well, in which you have not called upon God to carry you through the day, in the exercise of a meek and lowly spirit.[18]

WILLIAM LAW

 SCRIPTURE MEMORY

MATTHEW 11:29-30—*Take my yoke upon you. Let me teach you, because I am humble and gentle at heart, and you will find rest for your souls. For my yoke is easy to bear, and the burden I give you is light.*

CHAPTER 11

DIVINE FELLOWSHIP

Just as you accepted Christ Jesus as your Lord, you must continue to follow him. Let your roots grow down into him, and let your lives be built on him. Then your faith will grow strong in the truth you were taught, and you will overflow with thankfulness.

COLOSSIANS 2:6-7

Joy is the sign that God is everything to you.

ANDREW MURRAY, *Power in Prayer*

WHEN GOD IS ENOUGH FOR us, one of the significant blessings we experience is the joy of having personal fellowship with our Lord. Learning of God's great love and sacrifice on our behalf should create in us an ardent desire to grow in our relationship with Him. If we are yoked to Christ, our hearts should be filled with the joy of treasured fellowship with Him day after day. Paul, having realized the grace and completeness of Christ, declared that "everything else is worthless when compared with the infinite value of knowing Christ Jesus my Lord" (Philippians 3:8). Our final chapter in this study is meant to encourage and strengthen us to maintain zealously our walk with the Lord. We must let our roots grow down deep into Christ. Charles Spurgeon asked this compelling question concerning our relationship with the Lord: "Why should every year not be richer than the last in love, usefulness, and joy; for I am nearer the celestial hills, I have more experience with my Lord, and I should be more like Him?"[1]

Indeed, why not? God is the great Giver of all things and we, as His grateful children, should bow in humility before our blessed Lord and worship Him. Andrew Murray wrote,

> It takes time and deep reverence and adoring worship to come under the full impression that He who dwelleth in the glory of the Father, before whom all heaven bows in prostrate adoration, is none other than He who offers to be my companion, to lead me like a shepherd, who cares for each individual sheep, and so to make me one of those who follow the Lamb wherever He goes.[2]

❧ PARTICIPATING IN THE DIVINE RELATIONSHIP

1. Paul reminded the Corinthian church: "God is faithful, by whom you were called into the fellowship of his Son, Jesus Christ our Lord" (1 Corinthians 1:9, ESV). Andrew Murray noted that the Lord offers to be our companion. How do the following verses encourage you to deepen your relationship with the Lord?

   PSALM 27:8 ···

PSALM 84:1-4, 10-12 ·· ⌇

JOHN 15:5 ·· ⌇

2. Scripture describes some exceptional, miraculous, and life-changing encounters with God. The purpose in reading these Scriptures is not to think that we must experience God in these exact ways, but to be assured that God does speak to us through His Spirit and His Word. Our part is to be attuned to hear Him. Describe how these encounters bless and encourage you as you participate in your divine relationship with the Lord.

GENESIS 17:1-6 ·· ⌇

GENESIS 32:22-28 ·· ⌇

EXODUS 3:1-6 ·· ⌇

JOSHUA 5:13-15 ·· ∾

———————— ∾ ————————

More than anything else, Jacob wanted the blessing of the Lord on his life, and for this holy desire, he's to be commended. But before we can begin to be like the Lord, we have to face ourselves and admit what we are in ourselves. That's why the Lord asked him, "What is your name?" As far as the Genesis record is concerned, the last time Jacob was asked that question, he told a lie! His father asked, "Who are *you, my son?" and Jacob said to his father, "I* am *Esau your firstborn" (27:18-19, NKJV). The Lord didn't ask the question in order to get information, because He certainly knew Jacob's name and that Jacob had the reputation of being a schemer and a deceiver. "What is your name?" meant, "Are you going to continue living up to your name, deceiving yourself and others, or will you admit what you are and let Me change you?" In the Bible, receiving a new name signifies making a new beginning and this was Jacob's opportunity to make a fresh start in life.*[3]

WARREN WIERSBE

3. Isaiah wrote these convincing words: "The LORD must wait for you to come to him so he can show you his love and compassion" (Isaiah 30:18). It is our responsibility to take steps to be intimate with the Lord. What can you discover from these verses about what might hinder your growth and time with God?

MARK 4:18-19 ··

1 CORINTHIANS 3:1-3 ··

HEBREWS 5:12-14 ··

4. Oswald Chambers observed, "It is a joy to Jesus when a disciple
    takes time to step more intimately with Him."[4] Express your
    thoughts about God's longing to have a relationship with you
    and what steps you can take to have a stronger faith and life
    built on Him.

We are called to an everlasting preoccupation with God.[5]

A. W. TOZER

⚘ CULTIVATING THE DIVINE RELATIONSHIP

5. William Howells reminds us, "Do not be content with swimming on the surface of divine truth; make it your element; *dive* into it."[6] Record the highlights of the heartfelt prayers for intimacy found in these Scriptures.

EXODUS 33:13 • *Moses* ....⌒

PSALM 63:1 ....⌒

PSALM 90:14 ....⌒

PSALM 119:33-40 ....⌒

———————— ∽ ————————

Man needs to be alone with God. *Without this, God
cannot have the opportunity to shine into his heart, to
transform his nature by His divine working, to take
possession and to fill him with the fullness of God.*[7]

ANDREW MURRAY

6. The Word and prayer are indispensable in establishing firm,
    deep roots in Christ. What can you learn about spending time
    with God from these passages?

    DEUTERONOMY 17:18-20 • *Guidelines not only for a king!*

    EZRA 7:10

    MATTHEW 6:6

Dear child of God, let us never say, "I have no time for God." Let the Holy Spirit teach us that the most important, the most blessed, the most profitable time of the whole day is the time we spend alone with God. Pray to the Lord Jesus, who in His earthly life experienced the need of prayer; pray to the Holy Spirit, who will impress upon us this divine truth. As indispensable to me as the bread I eat, and the air I breathe, is communion with God through His Word and prayer. Whatever else is left undone, God has the first and chief right to my time. Then only will my surrender to God's will be full and unreserved.[8]

ANDREW MURRAY

7. Among the countless blessings of divine fellowship is the truth that He never leaves us or forsakes us. "Language . . . has created the word 'loneliness' to express the pain of being alone. And it has created the word 'solitude' to express the glory of being alone."[9] Growing in intimacy with Christ enables us to discern the difference between loneliness and solitude. How do these selected Scriptures encourage you to manage times of loneliness?

PSALM 61:1-5 ....

PSALM 68:3-6 ....

For this loneliness, this place in our hearts that no other human being can touch, is the place reserved for God alone, the place that only He can fill. No human being can love us as God does. No other person can speak to us from the bottom of our own hearts as the Holy Spirit does. No one else can plumb the mystery of our character and discern our peculiar needs and gifts as clearly as we ourselves can, by the Spirit's light. Accordingly, all of us must discover what it means to have no other comfort except the comfort that we ourselves can draw from our God in the lonely privacy of our own prayers.[10]

MIKE MASON

 ## SCRIPTURAL RESPONSES TO GOD'S SUFFICIENCY

When God Didn't Seem to Be Enough

THE RICH YOUNG MAN

As Jesus was starting out on his way to Jerusalem, a man came running up to him, knelt down, and asked, "Good Teacher, what must I do to inherit eternal life?" "Why do you call me good?" Jesus asked. "Only God is truly good. But to answer your question, you know the commandments: 'You must not murder.

You must not commit adultery. You must not steal. You must not testify falsely. You must not cheat anyone. Honor your father and mother.'" "Teacher," the man replied, "I've obeyed all these commandments since I was young." Looking at the man, Jesus felt genuine love for him. "There is still one thing you haven't done," he told him. "Go and sell all your possessions and give the money to the poor, and you will have treasure in heaven. Then come, follow me." At this the man's face fell, and he went away sad, for he had many possessions.

MARK 10:17-22

When God Was Enough

MARY OF BETHANY

As Jesus and the disciples continued on their way to Jerusalem, they came to a certain village where a woman named Martha welcomed him into her home. Her sister, Mary, sat at the Lord's feet, listening to what he taught. But Martha was distracted by the big dinner she was preparing. She came to Jesus and said, "Lord, doesn't it seem unfair to you that my sister just sits here while I do all the work? Tell her to come and help me." But the Lord said to her, "My dear Martha, you are worried and upset over all these details! There is only one thing worth being concerned about. Mary has discovered it, and it will not be taken away from her."

LUKE 10:38-42

8. Certainly Christ's direction to the rich man is not to be applied to everyone. This young man had a superficial view of Jesus and a good-works approach to salvation. Nonetheless, he allowed the seed of God's Word to fall among the thorns, and he let the lure of wealth and the desire for other

things keep him from following the Lord. What can you learn from the rich young man and Mary of Bethany about the importance of choosing to fix your heart fully on Christ in order to follow Him?

THOUGHTS AND REFLECTIONS FROM AN OLDER WOMAN

Truly, one of the crowning discoveries—the last and greatest lesson that the soul has to learn—is to know that God is enough. We have studied this lesson in the school of Christ these past few weeks, and we have learned the completeness and sufficiency of our almighty God who loves, sacrifices, gives, and desires to be preeminent in our lives. We no longer have to seek for fulfillment or live in fear. We have a Shepherd who graciously provides for all our needs and guides us individually on the best path. We are confident and at peace that God is continually working on our behalf to conform us to Christ. And it is in this conformity to Christ that we become who He wants us to be. Grounded in His sufficiency we can now be light, salt, and ambassadors for Him on whatever path He has placed us.

Because of God's gracious and wise sufficiency, we are no longer tempted to find satisfaction in counterfeit gods that offer momentary gratification and leave us empty and searching for more. We are freed from the arrogance of living independently—forever carrying the weight of protecting and providing for ourselves—believing that we know best. We are caught up in the great "I Am" and are at peace that God's ways are right and good even when He is not the God we would prefer Him to be. We are convinced of God's love and faithfulness in sending His Son to die for us. We cling to the great truth of redemption and live by faith through the storms that assail us, knowing that God never leaves us or forsakes us.

We live expectantly, seeking God's will for each day, knowing that He will guide us in the path that will bring Him glory. We experience the rare jewel of contentment because God is a wise and loving Father who bestows "an inner sufficiency that keeps us at peace in spite of outward circumstances."[11] We humbly take the yoke of Christ in order to become like Him. We consider it a high privilege to sacrifice time, service, and the demands of the world to deepen our fellowship with the Lord.

God is *El Shaddai*, the almighty God. As our Creator-Redeemer-Immanuel, He has proven that He is for us by His unfailing love and personal involvement in our lives. His grace and presence are enough for any need, any trial, any circumstance, any sickness, any hurt, any moment. He is the only One who is constant, faithful, and able to rescue and redeem our suffering. He desires relationship and intimacy with His children. He is an all-sufficient, all-powerful, all-loving, all-sovereign God, and He wants to prove to us that He is indeed enough. "Since he did not spare even his own Son but gave him up for us all, won't he also give us everything else?" (Romans 8:32).

Annie Johnson Flint wrote the hymn "He Giveth More Grace." Here is the chorus:

His love has no limit,
His grace has no measure,
His power has no boundary known unto men;
For out of His infinite riches in Jesus,
He giveth, and giveth, and giveth again![12]

How blessed you are to be God's child who can continually receive His limitless love, His immeasurable grace, His boundless power, and His fathomless riches. Trust and rest in God's sufficiency. Take His yoke. Clothe yourself in humility. Set your heart to learn contentment. Let your roots go down deep into the Lord. Keep your hand in His and continue your journey with great joy because you have made the crowning discovery that God, and God alone, is enough.

PERSONAL THOUGHTS AND REFLECTIONS

Still your heart and focus your thoughts on the Lord by praying these verses:

> Your unfailing love is better than life itself;
> how I praise you!
> I will praise you as long as I live,
> lifting up my hands to you in prayer.
> You satisfy me more than the richest feast.
> I will praise you with songs of joy.

PSALM 63:3-5

9. Take time to review your personal reflections for each chapter. Make a note of the significant truths that were impressed on your heart.

10. Summarize what this study has meant to you and how you hope your life will change.

11. As you look over your truths, write down at least two or three that you sense the Lord wants you to pray over and apply to your life. Write down some ways for implementing these truths into your life.

12. How would you describe a woman who knows that God is enough?

13. Colossians 2:7 states that as a result of the truth you have been taught, "You will overflow with thankfulness." As you reflect on this study, express your thankfulness to God for all He has taught you.

14. Close your time with the Lord by letting Him know your desire to be His woman who testifies by her life that He is enough. Let Him know of your commitment to stay yoked to Christ and of your resolve to deepen your intimacy with Him. Ask Him to guard your heart, increase your faith, and mold you into the image of Christ. Humbly bow before Him and praise Him that all His dealings are meant to teach you that He is enough. Praise Him for not sparing His own Son but for giving Him up for you and for His continued grace in giving you all things. Take time until you come under the full consciousness of an assured faith that as the almighty God, Christ will work for you and in you and through you all that God desires and all that you will ever need.

All fear is but the notion that God's love ends. Did you think I end, that My bread warehouses are limited, that I will not be enough? But I am infinite, child. What can end in Me? Can life end in Me? Can happiness? Or peace? Or anything you need? Doesn't your Father always give you what you need? I am the Bread of Life and My bread for you will never end. Fear thinks God is finite and fear believes that there is not going to be enough and hasn't counting one thousand gifts, endlessly counting gifts, exposed the lie at the heart of all fear? In Me, blessings never end because My love for you never ends. If My goodnesses toward you end, I will cease to exist, child. As long as there is a God in heaven, there is grace on earth and I am the spilling God of the uncontainable, forever-overflowing-love-grace.[13]

ANN VOSKAMP

SCRIPTURE MEMORY

COLOSSIANS 2:6-7—*Just as you accepted Christ Jesus as your Lord, you must continue to follow him. Let your roots grow down into him, and let your lives be built on him. Then your faith will grow strong in the truth you were taught, and you will overflow with thankfulness.*

The Father spoke:

My child?

Yes, Father. I am here—but I have little to say.

Are you content to be in My presence?

Yes. I am content to wait quietly before You—for I know that
You alone are my rock and my salvation.

What has changed?

A deeper understanding of who You are.

A fresh appreciation of how very much You are for me.

A clearer recognition of Your personal commitment to give me
what is best in light of eternity.

How will this knowledge change you?

I think it will take some time, but I sense a confidence and peace
that I have not had before. I believe that I finally know that
true rest and completeness can be found only in You and
You alone.

Do you now trust Me for who I AM?

Yes, I no longer want to doubt or question Your will for me or
seek satisfaction apart from You. I willingly take Your yoke
and trust You to choose for me and to provide for my needs.

And what do you desire?

I desire to be deeply rooted in You, to experience the richness of
Your divine fellowship, and to grow in faith and conformity
to Christ so that my life will exemplify that You, alone, are
enough for me.

*You have spoken well, My child. Your words bring Me much joy. Be
assured of My eternal presence and My everlasting provision for
all you need. You now know that I am your Jehovah-jireh who
will always be enough for you.*

About the Author

CYNTHIA HEALD IS A NATIVE Texan. She and her husband, Jack, a veterinarian by profession, are on staff with The Navigators in Tucson, Arizona. They have four children—Melinda, Daryl, Shelly, and Michael—as well as twelve grandchildren.

Cynthia graduated from the University of Texas with a BA in English. She frequently speaks at church women's seminars and conferences, both nationally and internationally.

She loves to be with her family, share the Word of God, have tea parties, and eat out.

BIBLE STUDIES, BOOKS, VIDEOS, AND AUDIOS
by Cynthia Heald

BIBLE STUDIES:
Becoming a Woman of Excellence
Becoming a Woman of Faith
Becoming a Woman of Freedom
Becoming a Woman of Grace
Becoming a Woman of Prayer
Becoming a Woman of Purpose
Becoming a Woman of Simplicity
Becoming a Woman of Strength
Becoming a Woman Who Loves
Becoming a Woman Whose God Is Enough
Intimacy with God
Walking Together (adapted from *Loving Your Husband* and *Loving Your Wife*,
    by Jack and Cynthia Heald)

BOOKS AND DEVOTIONALS:
Becoming a Woman Who Walks with God (a Gold Medallion–winning devotional)
Drawing Near to the Heart of God
Dwelling in His Presence
I Have Loved You
Maybe God Is Right After All
Promises to God
Uncommon Beauty

**VIDEO DOWNLOADS AND DVDS OF THE FOLLOWING STUDIES ARE
    AVAILABLE AT CYNTHIAHEALD.COM:**
Becoming a Woman of Excellence
Becoming a Woman of Simplicity
Becoming a Woman of Strength
Becoming a Woman Whose God Is Enough

**AUDIO DOWNLOADS OF THE FOLLOWING STUDIES ARE AVAILABLE
    AT CYNTHIAHEALD.COM:**
Becoming a Woman of Simplicity
Becoming a Woman of Strength
Becoming a Woman Whose God Is Enough

Notes

CHAPTER 1—GOD, THE CREATOR AND GIVER OF ALL THINGS

1. Blaise Pascal, in *Pensées*, http://christian-quotes.ochristian.com/Blaise-Pascal -Quotes/page-4.shtml.
2. John Baillie, *A Diary of Private Prayer* (New York: Scribner, 1949), 57.
3. Mike Mason, *The Gospel According to Job* (Wheaton, IL: Crossway, 1994), 392.
4. Allen P. Ross, in *The Bible Knowledge Commentary: Old Testament*, eds. John F. Walvoord and Roy B. Zuck (Wheaton, IL: Victor, 1985), 29.
5. Augustine, in *The Treasury of Christian Spiritual Classics*, introduction by Timothy P. Weber (Nashville: Nelson, 1994), 11.
6. S. R. Aldridge, in *The Pulpit Commentary*, eds. H. D. M. Spence and Joseph S. Exell, vol. 18, Romans (Peabody, MA: Hendrickson, n.d.), 253.
7. Charles H. Spurgeon, *Morning and Evening: An Updated Edition of the Classic Devotional in Today's Language*, ed. Roy H. Clarke (Nashville: Nelson, 1994), October 16, evening.
8. Warren W. Wiersbe, *The Wiersbe Bible Commentary: Old Testament* (Colorado Springs: Cook Communications, 2007), 27.
9. Reinhold Niebuhr, in *A Praying Life* by Paul E. Miller (Colorado Springs: NavPress, 2009), 125.
10. A. W. Tozer, *The Pursuit of God* (ReadAClassic.com, 2012), 41.
11. Julian of Norwich, in *Prayers Across the Centuries* (Wheaton, IL: Harold Shaw, 1993), 80.
12. Charles H. Brent, in *The Pursuit of God: A 31-Day Experience* by A. W. Tozer, comp. Edythe Draper (Camp Hill, PA: WingSpread Publishers, 1995), 107.
13. D. Martyn Lloyd-Jones, *The All-Sufficient God* (Carlisle, PA: Banner of Truth Trust, 2005), 70.

CHAPTER 2—GOD, OUR ALL-SUFFICIENT SHEPHERD

1. Phillip Keller, *A Shepherd Looks at Psalm 23* (Grand Rapids, MI: Zondervan, 1970), 17.

2. Hannah Whitall Smith, *The God of All Comfort*, (Chicago: Moody, 1956), 80.

3. Robert Jamieson, A. R. Fausset, and David Brown, *Commentary Practical and Explanatory on the Whole Bible* (Grand Rapids, MI: Zondervan, 1961), 1312.

4. C. S. Lewis, in *The Pursuit of God: A 31-Day Experience* by A. W. Tozer, comp. Edythe Draper (Camp Hill, PA: WingSpread Publishers, 1995), 106.

5. W. F. Adeney, in *The Pulpit Commentary*, eds. H. D. M. Spence and Joseph S. Exell, vol. 20, Philippians (Peabody, MA: Hendrickson, 1985), 198–99.

6. Matthew Henry, *Matthew Henry's Commentary on the Whole Bible*, vol. 3 (Peabody, MA: Hendrickson, 1985), 560.

7. Charles H. Spurgeon, *The Treasury of David*, vol. 1, part 2 (McLean, VA: MacDonald Publishing, n.d.), 171.

8. C. S. Lewis, *Letters to Malcolm: Chiefly on Prayer* (New York: Harcourt, 1964), 28.

9. Spurgeon, *The Treasury of David*, vol. 2, 446.

10. Charles H. Spurgeon, *The Power of Prayer in a Believer's Life*, ed. Robert Hall (Lynnwood, WA: Emerald Books, 1993), 109–10.

11. Annie Dillard, in *The Westminster Collection of Christian Quotations*, comp. Martin H. Manser (Louisville, KY: Westminster, 2001), 295.

12. Spurgeon, *The Treasury of David*, vol. 1, Psalm 23, 354.

CHAPTER 3—GOD, WHO IS FOR US AND NOT AGAINST US

1. Warren W. Wiersbe, *The Wiersbe Bible Commentary: New Testament* (Colorado Springs: Cook Communications, 2007), 431.

2. Robert L. Saucy, in *The Portable Seminary*, ed. David Horton (Bloomington, MN: Bethany, 2006), 93.

3. Wayne Grudem, *Systematic Theology: An Introduction to Biblical Doctrine* (Grand Rapids, MI: Zondervan, 1994), 255–56.

4. Saucy, 90.

5. A. W. Tozer, *The Knowledge of the Holy* (New York: Harper & Row, 1961), 42.

6. Oswald Chambers, *My Utmost for His Highest* (Westwood, NJ: Barbour and Co., 1935), June 9.

7. Andrew Murray, *Power in Prayer* (Minneapolis: Bethany, 2011), 18.

8. Timothy Keller, *The Reason for God* (New York: Dutton, 2008), 197.

9. Wiersbe, 431.

10. Philip Yancey, *Disappointment with God* (Grand Rapids, MI: Zondervan, 2009), 186.

11. Andrew Murray, *Daily Secrets of Christian Living*, comp. Al Bryant (Minneapolis: Bethany, 1978), March 11.

12. Carlo Corretto, in *A Guide to Prayer for Ministers and Other Servants* by Reuben P. Job and Norman Sawchuck (Nashville: Upper Room Publishers, 1983), 15.

CHAPTER 4—SEEKING SATISFACTION IN IDOLS

1. John Phillips, *The John Phillips Commentary Series: Exploring the Epistles of John* (Grand Rapids, MI: Kregel, 2003), 185.

2. Augustine, in *The Treasury of Christian Spiritual Classics,* introduction by Timothy P. Weber (Nashville: Nelson, 1994), 11.
3. George Rawlinson, in *The Pulpit Commentary,* eds. H. D. M. Spence and Joseph S. Exell, vol. 1, Exodus, vol. 2 (Peabody, MA: Hendrickson, 1985), 131.
4. Warren W. Wiersbe, *The Wiersbe Bible Commentary: Old Testament* (Colorado Springs: Cook Communications, 2007), 1110.
5. Eugene Peterson, Introduction to Ecclesiastes in *The Message* (Colorado Springs: NavPress, 2005), 882.
6. Keller, *Counterfeit Gods* (New York: Riverhead Books, 2009), 23.
7. Ibid., xx.
8. Warren W. Wiersbe, *The Wiersbe Bible Commentary: New Testament* (Colorado Springs: Cook Communications, 2007), 59.
9. Charles H. Spurgeon, *Morning and Evening: An Updated Edition of the Classic Devotional in Today's Language,* ed. Roy H. Clarke (Nashville: Nelson, 1994), March 7, evening.
10. John Phillips, The John Phillips Commentary Series: *Exploring Colossians & Philemon* (Grand Rapids, MI: Kregel, 2002), 119.
11. D. Young, in *The Pulpit Commentary,* eds. H. D. M. Spence and Joseph S. Exell, vol. 1, Exodus, vol. 2 (Peabody, MA: Hendrickson, 1985), 146.
12. Keller, 20.
13. John Wesley, in *The Westminster Collection of Christian Quotations,* comp. Martin H. Manser (Louisville, KY: Westminster, 2001), 186.
14. George Mueller, in *Streams in the Desert* by L. B. Cowman (Grand Rapids, MI: Zondervan, 1997), 277.

CHAPTER 5—BEING SATISFIED WITH SELF
1. Oswald Chambers, *My Utmost for His Highest* (Westwood, NJ: Barbour and Co., 1935), June 12.
2. Ibid., November 28.
3. Lawrence O. Richards, *Expository Dictionary of Bible Words* (Grand Rapids, MI: Zondervan, 1985), 76.
4. Beth Moore, *Praying God's Word* (Nashville: Broadman, Holman, 2000), 57.
5. Timothy Keller, *Counterfeit Gods* (New York: Riverhead Books, 2009), 88.
6. Ibid., 88–89.
7. Charles H. Spurgeon, *Morning and Evening: An Updated Edition of the Classic Devotional in Today's Language,* ed. Roy H. Clarke (Nashville: Nelson, 1994), June 3, evening.
8. John Stott, *The Radical Disciple* (Nottingham, England: InterVarsity, 2010), 27.
9. Oliver Wendell Holmes Jr., in *Never Scratch a Tiger with a Short Stick,* comp. Gordon S. Jackson (Colorado Springs: NavPress, 2003), 86.
10. J. Marshall Lang, in *The Pulpit Commentary,* eds. H. D. M. Spence and Joseph S. Exell, vol. 16, Luke (Peabody, MA: Hendrickson, 1985), 117.

11. Andrew Murray, *Humility* (Minneapolis: Bethany House, 2001), 16–17.
12. C. S. Lewis, *Mere Christianity* (San Francisco: HarperSanFrancisco, 1980), 125.
13. Chambers, June 17.

CHAPTER 6—TAKING OFFENSE

1. Albert Barnes, *Barnes' Notes: Notes on the New Testament*, ed. Robert Frew, Matthew (Grand Rapids, MI: Baker, 1998), 118.
2. Henri J. M. Nouwen, *The Return of the Prodigal Son* (New York: Doubleday, 1994), 104.
3. Timothy Keller, *The Prodigal God* (New York: Riverhead Books, 2008), 12–13.
4. Nouwen, 36.
5. Keller, 86–87.
6. Ibid., xvii.
7. Oswald Chambers, *My Utmost for His Highest* (Grand Rapids, MI: Discovery House, 1992), October 5.
8. Erwin W. Lutzer, *Where Was God?* (Carol Stream, IL: Tyndale, 2006), 39.
9. Philip Yancey, *Disappointment with God* (Grand Rapids, MI: Zondervan, 1988), 115.
10. Elisabeth Elliot, *These Strange Ashes* (Ann Arbor, MI: Servant, 1998), 125–26.
11. Ibid., 127.
12. Chambers, March 15.
13. Randy Alcorn, "The Sentence Against God," Eternal Perspective Ministries, March 22, 2013, www.epm.org./blog/2013/Mar/22/sentence.
14. Mike Mason, *The Gospel According to Job* (Wheaton, IL: Crossway, 1994), 388.
15. W. Clarkson, in *The Pulpit Commentary*, eds. H. D. M. Spence and Joseph S. Exell, vol. 16, Luke (Peabody, MA: Hendrickson, 1985), 56.

CHAPTER 7—HAVING LITTLE FAITH

1. B. C. Caffin, in *The Pulpit Commentary*, eds. H. D. M. Spence and Joseph S. Exell, vol. 15, Matthew (Peabody, MA: Hendrickson, 1985), 336.
2. Matthew Henry, *Matthew Henry's Commentary on the Whole Bible*, vol. 5, (Peabody, MA: Hendrickson, 1985), n.p.
3. Henry Blackaby and Richard Blackaby, from *Experiencing God* in *How Great Is Our God* (Colorado Springs: NavPress, 2011), 70.
4. D. Martyn Lloyd-Jones, *The All-Sufficient God* (Carlisle, PA: Banner of Truth Trust, 2005), 72.
5. Charles Spurgeon, http://thinkexist.com/quotes/Charles_H._Spurgeon.
6. Oswald Chambers, *My Utmost for His Highest* (Westwood, NJ: Barbour and Co., 1935), October 31.
7. W. Clarkson, in *The Pulpit Commentary*, eds. H. D. M. Spence and Joseph S. Exell, vol. 16, Luke (Peabody, MA: Hendrickson, 1985), 99.
8. C. S. Lewis, *The Problem of Pain* (Nashville: Broadman, Holman, 1996), 47–48.

9. Philip Yancey, *Disappointment with God* (Grand Rapids, MI: Zondervan, 2009), 201.

10. A. W. Tozer, *The Knowledge of the Holy* (New York: Harper & Row, 1961), 68.

11. Elisabeth Elliot, *On Asking God Why* (Old Tappan, NJ: Revell, 1989), 138.

12. Max Lucado, *In the Grip of Grace* (Dallas: Word, 1996), 132.

13. From a broadsheet in the British Museum, quoted in *The Treasury of David*, vol. 1, Psalm 27 (McLean, VA: MacDonald Publishing, n.d.), 12.

14. Oswald Chambers, *The Quotable Oswald Chambers*, comp. and ed. David McCasland (Grand Rapids, MI: Discovery House, 2008), 95.

15. Lewis, 43.

CHAPTER 8—GOD CHOOSES FOR YOU

1. A. W. Tozer, *The Knowledge of the Holy* (New York: Harper & Row, 1961), 69.

2. Jim Elliot, http://www.brainyquote.com/quotes/quotes/j/jimelliot189251.html.

3. Chambers, *My Utmost for His Highest* (Westwood, NJ: Barbour and Co., 1935), April 29.

4. Oswald Chambers, *My Utmost for His Highest: An Updated Edition in Today's Language*, ed. James Reimann (Grand Rapids, MI: Discovery House, 1992), August 5.

5. Henry Law, *Daily Prayer and Praise: The Book of Psalms Arranged for Private and Family Use*, vol. 2 (Carlisle, PA: Banner of Truth Trust, 2000), 260.

6. Warren W. Wiersbe, *The Wiersbe Bible Commentary: The Complete Old Testament in One Volume* (Colorado Springs: Cook Communications, 2007), 1097.

7. Frances Ridley Havergal, in *Streams in the Desert* by L. B. Cowman (Grand Rapids, MI: Zondervan, 1997), 425.

8. Chambers, *My Utmost for His Highest: An Updated Edition in Today's Language*, August 10.

9. Chambers, *My Utmost for His Highest: An Updated Edition in Today's Language*, May 25.

10. Mike Mason, *The Gospel According to Job* (Wheaton, IL: Crossway, 1994), 356.

11. F. B. Meyer, in *Streams in the Desert* by L. B. Cowman, 25.

CHAPTER 9—CONTENTMENT

1. Jeremiah Burroughs, *The Rare Jewel of Christian Contentment* (Carlisle, PA: Banner of Truth Trust, 2005), 28.

2. Warren Wiersbe, *The Wiersbe Bible Commentary: The Complete New Testament* (Colorado Springs: Cook Communications, 2007), 767.

3. Tim Challies, "The Essential: Idolatry," *challies.com* (blog), December 30, 2012, http://www.challies.com/articles/the-essential-idolatry.

4. Jerry Bridges, *The Discipline of Grace* (Colorado Springs: NavPress, 1994), 131.

5. Elisha Galotti, "True Contentment," *The Galottis* (blog), October 18, 2012, http://www.thegalottis.com/2012/10/true-contentment.html.

6. Evelyn Underhill, in *The New Book of Christian Quotations*, comp. Tony Castle (New York: Crossroad, 1989), 136.

7. Burroughs, 90.

8. Hudson Taylor, quoted in *The Red Sea Rules* by Robert J. Morgan (Nashville: Nelson, 2001), 21.

9. C. S. Lewis, *Reflections on the Psalms* (New York: Harvest/Harcourt, 1958), 96–97.

10. Epictetus, in *Worth Repeating*, ed. Bob Kelly (Grand Rapids, MI: Kregel, 2003), 65.

11. Burroughs, 86–87.

12. Ibid., 91.

13. Samuel Storms, *Pleasures Evermore* (Colorado Springs: NavPress, 2000), 210.

14. Timothy Keller, *Counterfeit Gods* (New York: Riverhead Books, 2009), 19.

CHAPTER 10—HUMILITY

1. Warren Wiersbe, *The Wiersbe Bible Commentary: The Complete New Testament* (Colorado Springs: Cook Communications, 2007), 34.

2. *Random House Kernerman Webster's College Dictionary*, copyright © 2010, http://www.thefreedictionary.com/humility.

3. Wiersbe, 19.

4. Thomas Aquinas, in *Humility* by Andrew Murray (Minneapolis: Bethany, 2001), 13.

5. Barbara Madison, a friend, quoted from her letter to her grandchildren after being diagnosed with cancer, 2008.

6. Murray, 63.

7. Dwight L. Moody, *The Overcoming Life*, "Humility," http://christianbookshelf.org/moody/the_overcoming_life/humility.htm.

8. Anonymous, in *Streams in the Desert* by L. B. Cowman (Grand Rapids, MI: Zondervan, 1977), 277.

9. John Chrysostom, http://christian-quotes.ochristian.com/John-Chrysostom-Quotes/page-2.shtml.

10. Gary Inrig, *Quality Friendship: The Risks and Rewards* (Chicago: Moody, 1981), 168.

11. G. K. Chesterton, quoted in *Never Scratch a Tiger with a Short Stick*, ed. Gordon S. Jackson (Colorado Springs: NavPress, 2003), 85.

12. Anonymous, http://christian-quotes.ochristian.com/Humility-Quotes/.

13. Louis Evely, quoted in *The Pursuit of God: A 31-Day Experience* by A. W. Tozer (Camp Hill, PA: WingSpread Publishers, 1995), 202.

14. William Law, in *The Problem of Pain* by C. S. Lewis (Nashville: Broadman, Holman; 1996), 49.

15. Saint Cyran, quoted in *The New Dictionary of Thoughts: A Cyclopedia of Quotations* (New York: Standard, 1961), 500.

16. Meryl Streep, quoted in *Treasury of Women's Quotes*, comp. Carolyn Warner (Englewood Cliffs, NJ: Prentice-Hall, 1992), 41.

17. Anonymous, quoted in *Worth Repeating*, ed. Bob Kelly, (Grand Rapids, MI: Kregel, 2003), 176.

18. William Law, quoted in *The Westminster Collection of Christian Quotations,* comp. Martin H. Manser (Louisville, KY: Westminster, 2001), 182.

CHAPTER 11—DIVINE FELLOWSHIP

1. Charles Spurgeon, *Morning and Evening: An Updated Edition of the Classic Devotional in Today's Language*, ed. Roy H. Clarke (Nashville: Nelson, 1994), July 3 morning.

2. Andrew Murray, *Daily Secrets of Christian Living*, comp. Al Bryant, (Minneapolis: Bethany, 1978), May 6.

3. Warren W. Wiersbe, *The Wiersbe Bible Commentary: The Complete Old Testament in One Volume* (Colorado Springs: Cook Communicaitons, 2007), 110.

4. Oswald Chambers, *My Utmost for His Highest* (Grand Rapids, MI: Discovery House, 1992), January 7.

5. A. W. Tozer, *The Pursuit of God: A 31-Day Experience* (Camp Hill, PA: WingSpread Publishers, 1995), 8.

6. William Howells, quoted in *Words Old and New* by Horatius Bonar (Carlisle, PA: Banner of Truth Trust, 1994), 319.

7. Murray, April 8.

8. Murray, October 7.

9. Paul Tillich, http://www.brainyquote.com/quotes/quotes/p/paultillich107897 .html/.

10. Mike Mason, *The Gospel According to Job* (Wheaton, IL: Crossway, 1994), 229–30.

11. Warren Wiersbe, *The Wiersbe Bible Commentary: The Complete New Testament* (Colorado Springs: Cook Communications, 2007), 767.

12. Annie Johnson Flint, "He Giveth More Grace," in *Hymns for the Family of God* (Nashville: Paragon Associates, 1976), 112.

13. Ann Voskamp, *One Thousand Gifts* (Grand Rapids, MI: Zondervan, 2010), 161.

Become the Woman
God Created You to Be

978-1-60006-663-4
DVD 978-1-61521-821-9   978-1-57683-831-0

978-1-63146-564-2

978-1-61521-023-7

978-1-61521-021-3

A goal worth pursuing. Society beckons us to succeed—to achieve excellence in our appearance, our earning power, our family life. God Himself also beckons us to be women of excellence. But what exactly is He asking? If you're hungry for God's perspective on success, dig into God's Word with bestselling Bible teacher Cynthia Heald and experience the joy of becoming a woman of excellence.

Becoming a Woman of Grace
978-1-61521-022-0

Becoming a Woman of Strength
978-1-61521-620-8 | DVD 978-1-61747-902-1

Becoming a Woman of Freedom
978-1-57683-829-7

Becoming a Woman of Prayer
978-1-57683-830-3

**Becoming a Woman Whose
God Is Enough**
978-1-61291-634-7

Available wherever books are sold.   CP